A Season
of Rebirth

A Season
of Rebirth

Daily Meditations for Lent

Marc Foley

New City Press
Hyde Park, New York

In appreciation

To my dear friend
Sandra Gettings
for her editorial assistance

Published in the United States by New City Press
202 Cardinal Rd., Hyde Park, NY 12538
www.newcitypress.com
©2007 The Discalced Carmelites of the Immaculate Heart of Mary Province

Cover design by Durvanorte Correia

Library of Congress Cataloging-in-Publication Data:

Foley, Marc, 1949-
  A season of rebirth : daily meditations for Lent / Marc Foley.
       p. cm.
  Includes bibliographical references.
  ISBN-13 : 978-1-56548-256-2 (pbk.)
  1. Lent--Meditations.   I. Title
BV85 . F6125 2007
242' .34--dc22   2006025938

Printed in the United States of America

Table of Contents

Introduction 7

Ash Wednesday to Saturday 9

First Week of Lent 23

Second Week of Lent 45

Third Week of Lent 71

Fourth Week of Lent 91

Fifth Week of Lent 113

Holy Week 133

Notes 157

Works Cited 158

Introduction

April is the cruellest month, breeding
Lilacs out of the dead land ...
– T.S. Eliot, "The Waste Land"

Spring is a time of rebirth after a cruel death. It demands that the seed slumbering quietly in the earth suffer the violence of being split open. Aroused from its sleep, it is beckoned forth from its shell. Like the seed, we too are called forth from our protective shells. And we can grow only if we listen.

To listen is the primary act of obedience. Obedience, derived from the Latin *oboedire*, means *to listen*. And to truly listen involves a courageous openness and a readiness to change. If we are unwilling to change, then Lent has no point. For only in the new life offered to us at Easter do we find meaning in the dying of Lent.

Lent, derived from the Old English word *lencten,* means spring. Lent is a time of rebirth; it is a season to allow God's seed to germinate within us, a time to do those things necessary to break out of our self-centered, encapsulated lives into a new and more expansive life of love in Christ.

The following reflections invite us to ponder our lives and to open our listening hearts to the voice of God, so that Lent will truly be Lent — a spring that buds forth new life.

Ash Wednesday
to Saturday

Ash Wednesday

Matthew 6:1–6, 16–18

Jesus commends us to fast, to pray, and to give alms but cautions us not to perform these actions for the sake of acquiring a reputation for holiness.

In T.S. Eliot's play *Murder in the Cathedral,* Thomas à Becket is accosted by a temptation to martyrdom, that is, to win fame and glory by his death. When he realizes the nature of the temptation, he exclaims, "The last temptation is the greatest treason: To do the right deed for the wrong reason.... A Servant of God has chance of greater sin and sorrow, than the man who serves a king. For those who serve the greater cause may make the cause serve them" (44–45). Becket's words go to the heart of today's gospel. Giving alms, prayer, and fasting, all good deeds, may be done for the wrong reason. Acts meant to serve God may also serve our egos.

Deeds that serve God differ from those that serve our egos because of the *motive* that underlies them. As John Chrysostom comments upon today's gospel, "Since even if you should enter into your closet, and having shut the door, should do it for display, the doors will do you no good" ("Homilies on the Gospel of Saint Matthew" 132). We can draw as much attention to ourselves by standing in a corner as by basking in the limelight. In this regard, Jerome warns us, "Don't seek the fame of avoiding fame. Many who avoid having witnesses of their poverty, their tenderness of heart, their fasting, desire to win approval for the fact that they despise approval" (160–61). The motive out of which our choices arise is all-important because it determines the nature of our actions. If we give alms in order *to be known* to be generous, then our action is not a deed of generosity but of pride.

It matters little what we pride ourselves in because the lure of pride does not lie in the *object* of our pursuit but the *distinction* that it confers upon us. But, ultimately, the distinction that pride bestows betrays those who practice it. For whenever our pretense has evoked the praise of others, we become enslaved to the admiring audience that we have created. The Greek word translated in today's gospel as hypocrite (*hypokrites,* meaning actor) is instructive in this regard. Every actor knows that he is only as good as his last performance and stands in dread of a bad review. The more our self-esteem depends upon the opinion of others, the more insecure we become.

Being insecure in self-esteem is the core dynamic of what psychologists call a narcissistic personality disorder. This might strike us as strange because narcissists often project a grandiose persona of self-assurance. But their personas are fragile. Narcissists easily become depressed and full of self-doubt when they receive less than rave reviews for their performances. They are like kites. When the winds of approval and applause are favorable, narcissists fly high; when the winds of acclamation subside, they fall into the doldrums of despondency and despair.

Most of us have a narcissistic wound, for we are insecure in the knowledge that we are loved. So we go through life wearing masks, conning parts, playing roles, giving performances in the hope of winning love or at least curtailing disapproval. In this regard, we are all frightened hypocrites.

There is nothing wrong with *receiving* praise, but the more we *seek* it, the more we become addicted to it. Jesus is straightforward in what we must do. We must fast from any behavior that is designed to win the approval of others. Jesus' counsels to "go to your room and pray in secret ... keep your deeds of mercy secret ... groom your hair and wash your face when you fast" are but three examples.

Augustine writes that when we fast from our play-acting, we are "cleansing the eye by which God is seen" ("The Lord's Sermon on the Mount" 92). We cannot see our Father who dwells in secret if our minds are preoccupied with our performance. Saint Teresa tells us, "All harm comes to us from not keeping our eyes fixed on [God]" ("The Way of Perfection" 97). As we begin Lent, let us direct our gaze inward, to the God who dwells in secret and who loves us.

Thursday After Ash Wednesday

Deuteronomy 30: 15–20/Luke 9: 22–25

Jesus tells us that in order to follow him, we must deny our very selves. But this "denial" of self is in truth an acceptance of our deepest self. For when we love, we "choose life" (Dt 30: 19).

In a village lived a rabbi esteemed for his ability to see into the human heart. In the same village also lived an atheist who wished to expose the rabbi as a fraud. One day, the atheist saw an injured bird lying upon the ground. Picking it up he said to himself, "At last, I have my chance. I will go to the rabbi when he is surrounded by his admiring congregation and while holding the bird behind my back I will ask him, 'Rabbi, I have a bird in my hand. Is it alive or is it dead?' If he says that it is dead, I will show him that it is alive. However, if he says that it is alive, I will break the bird's neck and show him that it is dead. In either case, I will expose the rabbi as a fraud."

So as the rabbi's congregation had surrounded him in the town's square, listening to him and asking him questions, the atheist wormed his way through the crowd and asked, "Rabbi, I have a bird in my hand. Is it alive or is it dead?" The rabbi, gazing deeply into the man's eyes, discerned his evil intent. So he replied, "The answer is in your hands."

"I set before you today life and prosperity, death and diversity ... blessings and the curses. Choose life, then." The choice is in our hands. For each day life places in our path people whom we must choose either to love or not love.

Think of your capacity to love as a room in which you live. The room is small (ten by twelve feet) and spartanly furnished with an army cot, a small wooden desk, a chair, and a bare hundred-watt bulb hanging from the ceiling. One day you open the door of your room and look down the darkened corridor. You see light streaming out from beneath a door. You leave your room, and hearing the door lock behind you, you rush down the corridor. You open the door and stand in amazement. The room is twenty feet by twenty-five feet. It is carpeted, has a large desk, a queen-size bed, an easy chair, and two lamps with shades. After a few months in this room, you begin to feel cramped and anxious. So once again, you open the door and look down the darkened corridor. You see light streaming out from under another door. Once again, you rush down the corridor. Beyond your wildest expectations, the new dwelling place has a lavishly furnished living room with a bay window, a fully equipped kitchen, a spacious bedroom, and a complete bath. After a few months ...[1]

Paradoxically, the spiritual life demands that we lose our life in order to find it, or in Cardinal Newman's words, we must "risk upon Christ's word what *we have* for what *we have not* [italics added]" (299). To *deny* one's very self is to *affirm* one's deepest self. Faith bids us to leave the constricted circumference in which we live and embrace a more expansive life of love. This does not mean that we must leave our jobs, change our residences or go to the foreign missions. But it does mean that we change our behavior. It means that we become more expansive in acts of charity, for we cannot hope to follow Christ home to God without increasing our love for our neighbor.

The two great commandments grow in unison. The sixth century hermit Dorotheus of Gaza compares God to the hub of a wheel and us to its spokes. Because the spokes converge on the hub, the closer we travel to God the closer we come to one another. "This is the nature of love: to the extent that we distance ourselves from the center of the circle and do not love God, we distance ourselves from our neighbor; but if we love God, then the nearer we draw to him in love, the more we are united with our neighbor in love" (Clément 272).

Friday After Ash Wednesday

Matthew 9: 14–16

John the Baptist's disciples approach Jesus with the objection, "Why do we and the Pharisees fast often, but your disciples do not fast?" Jesus responds that it is not appropriate for his disciples to fast while he is still among them.

Today's gospel seems to focus on fasting, but it concerns itself more with two other issues. First, *why* do we engage in any particular behavior? Second, is the behavior *appropriate*? Let us take each issue in turn.

Why do we engage in any particular behavior?

"Why do we and the Pharisees fast often but your disciples do not fast?" This is not a question but a criticism that smolders with anger. Ask yourself this question. Why would you be angry with people who do not practice a form of asceticism that you do, since their choice has no negative consequences in your life? It neither imposes upon you nor deprives you of anything. So why be angry?

One possible answer is that when we feel forced to do something that we really don't want to do, we envy others who are not burdened by the false sense of obligation that weighs us down. This is akin to workaholics who resent people who are not driven. In their hearts, they condemn the less-driven as lazy and irresponsible. But in truth, workaholics are envious. They cannot relax without feeling guilty or feeling afraid of having their image as indefatigable workers tarnished. Likewise, some people engage in spiritual devotions simply because someone else has recommended them highly. They do not want to lose the esteem of these people, so they bind themselves to devotions that do not fit the unique contours of their souls.

All of us are unique and must follow our own path. When Saint Thérèse was novice mistress, she described working with her novices in this fashion: "It is absolutely necessary to forget one's likings, one's personal conceptions, and to guide souls along the road which Jesus has traced out for them without trying to make them walk my own path.... There are really more differences among souls than there are among faces" (238–40).

In the same vein, Abbé de Tourville wrote, "Thomas Aquinas says that the angels differ as much from one another as if they belonged to different species. This is equally true of each one of us.... One of the hardest but one of the most absolutely necessary things is to follow our own particular line of development, side by side with souls who have a different one; often one opposed to our own.... We must be ourselves and not try to get inside someone else's skin. David could have done nothing in the armor of Saul; he refused it and ran to fetch his sling.... We must follow our own light as though we were alone in the world ... we must never be deflected from our own path" (26–28).

The Appropriateness of our Behavior

"The wedding guests cannot mourn as long as the bridegroom is with them, can they?" It is neither appropriate nor proper to fast at a wedding. To do so not only would indicate inordinate attachment to one's ascetical practice, but would also be rude. Thomas Aquinas asks whether a lack of mirth can be sinful. His response is, "Yes." Thomas writes that such a person becomes "burdensome to others, by offering no pleasure to others, and by hindering their enjoyment ... they are boorish and rude" (II, II, Q. 168, art. 4).

The appropriateness of our behavior is a matter of charity, as this story from the desert illustrates. "Once two brethren came to a certain elder whose practice it was to eat every other day. But when he saw the brethren, he joyfully invited them to dine with him, saying: 'Fasting has its reward, but he who eats out of charity fulfils two commandments, for he sets aside his own will and he refreshes his hungry brethren'" (Merton 77).

The appropriateness of when, where, and how we exercise any ascetical practice or virtue is important in the spiritual life. Francis de Sales wrote, "To insist on performing acts of a particular chosen virtue on every possible occasion is a great defect, as in the case of certain ancient philosophers who wished to be always weeping or always laughing; and still worse, to criticize and blame those who do not do the same. But Saint Paul says, 'Rejoice with those who rejoice, mourn with the mourners'" (85).

Saturday After Ash Wednesday

Luke 5: 27–32

Levi, the tax collector, is called by Jesus to leave his old life behind.

Levi was rich. Collecting taxes had brought him wealth, but had alienated him from society. Tax collectors were opportunists; they worked for the Romans; they abused their power, engaged in graft and extortion, and milked their own people dry. Ordinary citizens hated and ostracized them; they were excluded from the synagogue and assassinated by Zealots. Levi sat at his customs post *alone*. Like the figure in Gray's "Elegy," he had "shut the gates of mercy on mankind" and found himself outside the community, barred from human companionship and alienated from his own humanity.

Levi symbolizes the human condition. Namely, often when we obtain what we have striven for all of our lives we discover that we have become empty in the process. In his ground-breaking study of men in mid-life, Daniel Levinson found, "Often a man who has accomplished his goals comes to feel trapped: his success is meaningless and he is now caught in a stultifying situation" (31). Levinson cites Bertrand Russell as an example. For nine years, Russell slaved over his *magnum opus,* the *Principia Mathematica.* It won him the Nobel Prize, but in the process Russell became emotionally cold and estranged from his wife. "In the months after the book was completed, he realized that he was a great success as a philosopher and a failure as a human being" (31–32).

Russell's tragic experience is all too common. We begin our life's projects with the best intentions. But over time they snowball, taking on lives of their own. They begin to consume more and more of our time and energy, eventually eroding our humanity. When, like Levi or Russell, we find ourselves successful in the world but failures as human beings we finally face the truth.

When Levi got up and followed Jesus, he didn't so much leave everything behind as he attempted to regain what he had lost. The first step in being *found* is realizing that one is *lost.* Those in Twelve-Step programs know the truth of this statement, namely, that only when we have admitted that our lives have become empty and unmanageable do we come to believe that a Power greater than ourselves can restore us to sanity. Until we come to this point in our lives, we cling to the illusion of self-sufficiency. Levi's hitting rock bottom was a blessing in disguise, for his poverty disposed him to accept the gift of God's grace.

John Chrysostom writes that Jesus called Levi *while* he was sitting at his customs post in order "to indicate the power of God who called him. Levi [was not called *after* he] had forsaken this wicked trade but from the midst of the evils" ("Homilies on the Gospel of Saint Matthew" 199). This allowed Levi to realize that salvation is a pure gift. Levi arose from his customs post and followed Jesus. He became Matthew, a name meaning "gift of God."

First Week of Lent

Sunday

Cycle A: Genesis 2: 7–9, 3: 1–7

As we hear the story of the Fall in Genesis, the same question that God asked Adam confronts us: "Where are you?"

In a Hasidic story, an atheist persistently tried to catch the village rabbi in theological snares but always failed. One day the atheist asked, "Rabbi, is it true that God knows everything?" "Yes, my son," said the rabbi, "God knows everything." "Rabbi," the atheist continued, "is it also true that after The Fall, God asked Adam, 'Adam where are you?'" "Yes, my son, that is also true," the rabbi replied. The atheist smiled, thinking that he had finally caught the rabbi in a contradiction. "But rabbi," said the atheist, "If God knows everything, then why did God have to ask Adam where he was?" "My son," said the rabbi, "'Adam, where are you?' is not a question for *information* but for *reflection.*"

"Where am I?", a perennial question of life, encompasses many other questions. What am I doing with my life? Does it have any purpose or lasting significance? What does it all mean? These questions and those like them distill into one haunting question: When I come to die will it make any difference that I have ever lived? This question takes on a more somber hue the older we become. And if we ask ourselves what we must do for our life to have permanent significance, the answer is so simple that it evades us. We must live the one, unique life that God has entrusted to us.

There is another Hasidic story about rabbi Zossimus, who tried all of his life to be like Moses, David or one of the prophets. His inability to achieve his goal frustrated and depressed him. One night in a dream, an angel appeared to him and said, "At the last judgment, God will not ask you why you were not Moses or David but rather, why you were not Zossimus." God wanted Zossimus to do one thing — the same thing that he had asked Adam and Eve to do — tend the garden that was given to them and not to be deceived by unreality. "And you shall be like gods!" Tending the garden that God has entrusted to us, no matter how humble, is no mean and insignificant enterprise, for it affords numerous opportunities to love.

Each of us finds ourselves situated at a juncture of time, space, and circumstance unique to us alone; we are entrusted with opportunities to love to which no one else has been assigned. An old saying notes that there are many *occupations* in the Body of Christ but only one *vocation* — the vocation to love. Love is our true work no matter what our task; it is the only thing that gives our life ultimate and lasting significance. Regarding love, "Where are you?"

Sunday

Cycle B: Mark 1: 12–15

In the desert, Jesus is tempted by Satan and is ministered to by angels.

In the Hebrew language of the Old Testament, Satan means "The Adversary." He was part of the heavenly court, a heavenly prosecutor whose function was to question and test the genuineness of human virtue (e.g., see the opening chapter of the Book of Job). However, in the intertestimonial literature, Satan appears as a sinister character who hates humankind. In the New Testament, he is the Evil One, "the accuser of our brothers ... who night and day accused them before our God" (Rev 12:10). As accuser, Satan demands strict justice devoid of mercy. This is why Satan is a liar; he tells half-truths. He tries to rivet our minds on our sinfulness so that we become blind to God's mercy. He tries to make us submerge our souls in guilt and its attending sense of alienation so that we disbelieve the truth about our deepest identity — that we are God's beloved children.

At Jesus' baptism, the voice of God affirmed his deepest identity: "You are my beloved son." In the desert, Satan tried to make Jesus doubt what he had heard. But other voices in the desert assisted Jesus. "And angels ministered (Greek *diakomeo*) to him." *Diakomeo* means to serve, to care for, to support.

Is not the desert a symbol of our hearts? Does not the same dynamic operate in our lives that we see in the temptation story of Jesus? How often does the voice of self-doubt follow the voice of affirmation? How often does a voice within us seek to discredit any good that we find within ourselves? How often, after someone has given us positive feedback, do we say to ourselves, "She is only saying that to make me feel good"?

The sickness of soul that disposes us to believe the voices in our lives that criticize us more readily than those that affirm or support us is a deep wound that needs God's healing grace. Often, this grace comes late in life. In the *Purgatorio,* Dante's bathing in two rivers symbolizes his final purification and healing. The first river, *Lethe,* cleanses our minds from the guilt of sin. The second river, *Eunoe,* meaning Good Mind or Good Remembrance, resurrects from our unconscious all the submerged memories of our good deeds and God's love that sin and self-hate have repressed.

The voice of God's spirit within us is always trying to break through to consciousness, just as the heavens opened up at Jesus' baptism. We too need to hear God's affirming words. "You are my beloved son; you are my beloved daughter."

Sunday

Cycle C: Luke 4: 1–13

Satan tempts Jesus to turn stones into bread
and to worship the forces of evil in order to
acquire an earthly kingdom.

At the beginning of *Macbeth*, as Macbeth and
Banquo are riding home from war in the flush of
victory, three witches greet Macbeth with three ti-
tles. The first is his own title, "Thane of Glamis."
However the other two, "Thane of Cawdor" and
"King hereafter," belong to other men. Then the
witches vanish into thin air. As Macbeth and
Banquo continue their journey, a messenger from
the King meets them upon the road and bestows
upon Macbeth the title "Thane of Cawdor" as a reward for his valor in war. Macbeth is confused; he
knows that the Thane of Cawdor lives. But when
he learns that the King intends to execute the
Thane of Cawdor shortly for treason, Macbeth begins to tremble.

> Why do I yield to that suggestion
> Whose horrid image doth unfix my hair
> And make my seated heart knock at my ribs
> Against the use of nature?
> (1.3.147–49)

Why does Macbeth's murderous ambition to become king awaken? Since the witches' first prediction has come true, he sees the second as a real *possibility*. Possibility is the form of all temptation. We are not tempted in our weaknesses but in our strengths and talents. The charming are tempted to seduce others by their wiles because they know that they are likely to succeed; the knowledgeable are tempted to make an impressive show of their knowledge; bullies or those with strong personalities are tempted to intimidate others. Those who know how to manipulate another's guilt are tempted to make people do their bidding....

None of us has ever been tempted to turn stones into bread because we don't have the power to do so. It is not a possibility; therefore, it is not a temptation. The particular *forms* of Jesus' temptations are not our own, but *what* he was tempted with is the same — the abuse of power.

In one sense, all temptations are temptations of power, for power provides us with what we want, be it wealth, pleasure, possessions, prestige or revenge. Nothing entices us more than the possibility of getting our own way. But nothing corrupts us more than its pursuit. For the insatiable lust of getting what we want will not be satisfied until it devours our mind, heart, and will.

First Week of Lent

Monday

Leviticus 19: 1–2, 11–18
Matthew 25: 31–46

The Parable of the Last Judgment sets before us the primary consequence of our choices on this earth — the type of person we choose to become.

At the beginning of Oscar Wilde's *The Picture of Dorian Gray,* the protagonist, an exceptionally handsome young man, is standing before a portrait of himself that captures the full beauty of his youth. He begins to cry, for he knows that he will grow old and that his beauty will fade. So he makes a wild prayer that the portrait will suffer the inroads of time and bear the burden of his sins.

His prayer came true. Dorian's beauty did not fade, and the painting became a portrait of his soul. As he began to live a debauched and evil life, the portrait changed. A sneer of cruelty appeared at the corner of its lips, and over time, evil glared out from his eyes.

Dorian draped a cover over his portrait and locked it away in the attic of his house. Many years later, Dorian mounted the stairs and uncovered the portrait of his soul. What he saw was so hideous that he took a knife and slashed the painting. As he did so, he fell over dead. The next day, the butler went up into the attic. There he saw a slashed portrait of his master as he had last seen him, a man in the prime of youth. And lying dead on the floor beside the painting was a creature so hideous that he recognized it as Dorian Gray only by the rings upon his fingers.

Wilde's story is a parable of our lives. Each of us is engaged in the process of painting a self-portrait. Each choice is like a brush stroke. Every act of kindness or cruelty leaves its mark.

When we think of the Parable of the Last Judgment, the image of a court of law in which God renders justice, may come to our mind. But the last judgment is more like a masquerade ball at the stroke of midnight, at which time we must remove our masks and reveal our faces. What is revealed at that time will depend upon how we have lived.

The Greek word for judgment is *krisis,* which means "to reveal." The Last Judgment is the final disclosure of the person we have freely chosen to become. In *The Jerusalem Bible,* the King says to those on his left: "Go away from me, with *your* [italics added] curse upon you...." Hell is self-inflicted; it is not something that God imposes upon us. As Augustine once said, hell is God's final compliment upon our free will.

Today's first reading from Leviticus exhorts us to bear no hatred toward our neighbor or take revenge or cherish a grudge. We should heed these words in light of what we have said about judgment; for the only persons we really hurt are ourselves. If we hate, we become hateful persons; if we take revenge we become vengeful.

Tuesday

Matthew 6: 7–15

In the Our Father, we pray that God will not lead us into temptation. How can we interpret this puzzling petition?

Scripture scholar William Barclay knew a professor who, whenever he sat on a dissertation committee, regardless of the dissertation topic would ask the student, the following question: "Give me your interpretation of the petition in the Our Father, Lead us not into temptation but deliver us from evil." He asked this question for his own sake, for he had never heard an explanation that satisfied him. This petition is one of the most baffling passages in the New Testament. This petition is difficult to understand because the Greek word that is translated temptation (*peirasmos*) has more than one meaning. It can refer to a situation in which a person's mettle is *tested,* or it can mean *to tempt* in the sense of *to seduce.* Let us consider each meaning in turn.

Peirasmos translated as "a test"

Why would a person ask God to be delivered
from a situation that is an opportunity for spiritual
growth? Does not Saint James write, "Whenever
you face trials (*peirasmos*) of any kind, consider it
nothing but joy, because you know that the testing
of your faith produces endurance; and let endurance have its full effect, so that you may be mature
and complete, lacking in nothing" (Jas 1:2). Even
though we may all agree with Saint James' insight
that we grow by means of trials and tribulations,
don't we also want to be delivered from them?

John Chrysostom says that when we pray to
God, "lead us not into temptation but deliver us
from evil," we are praying to be delivered from
every form of harm. Some people may find this
interpretation too mundane. But is it? Rather, is
it not an expression of the most basic attitudes
that we should have in prayer — honesty and humility? Do not all of us want to be protected from
harm? Let us remember that Jesus who prayed to
his Father in the Garden of Gethsemane, "Not as
I will but as you will," also prayed, "If it is possible, let this cup pass me by." Since when is the
servant greater than his master?

Peirasmos translated as "to tempt"

In what sense can we even consider that God
would lead us into temptation? Grappling with
this question, Augustine wrote, "God does not *lead*
a man into temptation, but He suffers a man *to be
led* [italics added] into temptation when — through

First Week of Lent

one's just deserts — God leaves him bereft of divine aid" ("The Lord's Sermon on the Mount" 138). But why would God deprive a person of divine aid? How can we believe that God, who wants to save us from sin, would allow a person to fall into sin? We don't know. Thomas Aquinas gives one possible explanation. He taught that God will sometimes allow a soul to fall into serious sin in order to save it from something far worse — *pride*.

Wednesday

Jonah 3: 1–10

Jonah preaches repentance to the people of Nineveh but becomes bitter because he is successful.

Assyria had oppressed Israel cruelly. Jonah, who symbolizes Israel, represents certain Jews of his day who nursed a murderous grudge against Assyria and cultivated an intolerant nationalism that preached that God's mercy did not extend beyond Israel's borders. Within this context we can understand the central message of The Book of Jonah — condemnation of narrow-minded nationalism and proclamation of the universal largesse of God's mercy.

Our story begins with God telling Jonah to go to Nineveh and give them a warning — repent or be destroyed. In spite of Jonah's efforts to evade this commission, eventually he finds himself in Nineveh proclaiming God's message. The Ninevites repent and are preserved from destruction. This is what Jonah feared. At the end of the story, Jonah is bitter and angry because he wanted the Ninevites to be destroyed. He says to God, "This is why I fled to Tarshish.... I knew that you are a gracious God and merciful, slow to anger, and abounding in steadfast love, and ready to relent from punishing" (Jon 4:2). To give a warning to a hated foe was more than Jonah could bear. He could wreak revenge only by withholding God's saving word from them. Are we any different? How often do we withhold from others that which gives life — a word of kindness, a much deserved compliment, a word of encouragement?

Representing Israel, a nation brutalized by a tyrannical power, Jonah symbolizes the ultimate triumph of the oppressor. Viktor Frankl writes of this danger. After he had been liberated from Auschwitz, he noticed in some of the former inmates that "The only thing that had changed ... was that they were now the oppressors instead of the oppressed. They became instigators, not objects of willful force and injustice. They justified their behavior by their own terrible experiences. This was often revealed in apparently insignificant events. A friend was walking across a field with me toward the camp when suddenly we came to a field of green crops. Automatically, I avoided it, but he drew his arm through mine and dragged me through it. I stammered something about not treading down the young crops. He became annoyed, gave me an angry look and shouted, 'You don't say! And hasn't enough been taken from us? My wife and child have been gassed — not to mention everything else — and you would forbid me to tread a few stalks of oats!' Only slowly could these men be guided back to the commonplace truth that no one has the right to do wrong, not even if wrong has been done to him. We had to strive to lead them back to this truth, or the consequences would have been much worse than the loss of a few thousand stalks of oats. I can still see the prisoner who rolled up his shirt sleeves, thrust his right hand under my nose and shouted, 'May this hand be cut off if I don't stain it with blood on the day when I get home' " (*Man's Search for Meaning* 143–44).

All of us have suffered injustice and have been wronged by others. And we know the almost irresistible urge to seek revenge. Ultimately, though, the only person we injure is our self. Jonah's corrosive brooding is a sober warning to us all.

Thursday

Matthew 7:7–12

"Ask and you will receive." While God always answers our prayers, he does not always grant our requests.

In Somerset Maugham's autobiographical novel *Of Human Bondage,* young Philip Carey, a boy born with a clubfoot, prays that God will heal him. He wakes up the next morning to find that he has not been cured. His faith is shaken, for he has been told that whatever you ask for in prayer will be given. Throughout his life, Philip's deformity causes him much shame and humiliation, but it also brings about his transformation. At the very end of the novel, Philip comes to the following realization:

> And thinking over the long pilgrimage of his past, he accepted it joyfully. He accepted the deformity which had made his life so hard, but now he saw that by reason of it he had acquired that power of introspection which had given him so much delight. Without it he would never have had his keen appreciation of beauty, his passion for art and literature and his interest in the varied spectacle of life. The ridicule and contempt,

which had so often been heaped upon him, had turned his mind inward and called forth those flowers which he felt would never lose their fragrance. Then he saw that the normal was the rarest thing in the world. Everyone had some defect of body or of mind. He had thought of all the people he had known. He saw a long procession, deformed in body and warped in mind. At that moment he could feel a holy compassion for them all. He could pardon Griffiths for his treachery and Mildred for the pain she had caused him. The only reasonable thing was to accept the good of men and be patient with their faults. The words of the dying God crossed his memory: *Forgive them, for they know not what they do.* (680–81)

God always answers our prayers, but does not always grant our requests. We are promised that we will receive if we ask, but we are not told what will be given to us. The door will be opened to us, but we do not know what God has in store for us on the other side. We are told only that God knows *how* to give.

The ways of providence are mysterious indeed. Like Philip Carey, we should reflect upon the long pilgrimage of our past in order to apprehend the pattern of God's loving wisdom in our lives. Like Philip, we may realize what we once considered to have been our greatest curse was the occasion of our greatest blessing. We realize that what we once judged a stumbling block actually is a cornerstone. Conversely, think of how disastrously your life may have turned out had God granted your specific request.

Friday

Matthew 5: 20–26

Jesus warns: "If you are angry with a brother or sister you will be liable to judgment."

In today's gospel, Jesus seems to condemn anger, but precisely what is he condemning? Two Greek words are translated as anger in the New Testament — *thumos* and *orgizomai*. *Thumos* refers to a sudden outburst of anger, what we would call "flying off the handle." *Orgizomai*, on the other hand, suggests a deliberate element of thought; it names an anger that broods and is nurtured. William Blake's "A Poison Tree" captures *orgizomai:*

> I was angry with my friend:
> I told my wrath, my wrath did end.
> I was angry with my foe:
> I told it not, my wrath did grow.
> And I watered it in fears

Night and morning with my tears,
And I sunned it with smiles.
And with soft deceitful wiles.

And it grew both day and night,
Till it bore an apple bright,
And my foe beheld it shine,
And he knew that it was mine —

And into the garden stole
When the night had veiled the pole;
In the morning, glad, I see
My foe outstretched beneath the tree.
(129–30)

Jesus condemns anger, that broods and plots evil. *Orgizomai* is the word used in today's gospel. The real poison of Blake's poem is not in the apple but in the person who grew it; for anger that seethes and festers within us poisons our whole personality.

Jesus tells us, "Come to terms quickly with your accuser while you are on the way to court with him or your accuser may hand you over to the judge, and the judge to the guard, and you will be thrown into prison." In short, if you don't deal with your anger, it will deal with you. We all know the thick prison walls that anger erects — the tight neck muscles, the clenched jaw, the churning stomach. And worst of all, the fury-fed imagination that rants and raves incessantly and will not let us sleep. John Climacus writes, "Once, while engaged on some task, I happened to be sitting outside a monastery and near the cells of those living in solitude I could overhear them raging alone in their cells and in their bitter fury leaping about like caged partridges, leaping at the face of their offender as if he were actually there" (148). Does this scene seem strange? Do we not sometimes find ourselves alone, driving a car, sitting at our desk, taking a shower, caged in mind, castigating a foe or rehearsing a vitriolic scenario? And when our orgy of anger has burnt itself out, do we not feel exhausted and drained?

Realizing how anger imprisons us is a good place to begin to change. Rarely do we feel direct motivation to love the neighbor whom we hate. We have to begin with ourselves. Saint Bernard writes that we take the first step in charity when we love for *our own sake*. And we can love only one choice at a time.

Ernest Hemingway's approach in dealing with writers' block was as simple as his prose. He set for himself an attainable goal — write one true sentence. After he accomplished this task, he set for himself another goal — write one true sentence. Don't be unrealistic in trying to love your enemy. You may never be released completely from your prison of anger toward your neighbor. But you may be able to get weekend passes. Choose to do one act of kindness toward your enemy. And after you have accomplished your task, choose to do another.

42

Saturday

Matthew 5: 43–48

Jesus' exhortation to be perfect as our heavenly Father is perfect does not set an unrealistic goal, for it counsels us to be indiscriminate in our love.

"Be perfect, therefore, as your heavenly Father is perfect." Few lines in Scripture have engendered more despondency and scrupulosity than this one. Misinterpreted, this admonition to strive for perfection sets the bar so high that no one except God can clear it. Its Sisyphean nature dooms us to fail. Can anyone be as perfect as God is perfect?

We need to read the admonition to be perfect in today's gospel within context. Jesus is not telling us that we have to measure up to God; rather, we are called to be like God in a particular way — our charity should be indiscriminate. Our charity should be like the sun, which rises on the good and bad alike or the rain that falls upon the just and the unjust.

The sun and the rain cannot pick and choose upon whom they shine and shower. This inability to be selective is one way of understanding the old scholastic axiom, *bonum diffusivum sui* (the good is diffusive of itself). God's love is so overflowing and diffusive that it cannot be restrained.

It would be like telling someone who has just fallen in love, "Keep your happiness to yourself." It cannot be done. Their overabundance of joy compels lovers to share their happiness with everyone they meet. Similarly, think of God's love as the fragrance of a lilac bush. The bush cannot help but offer it to everyone who passes by. It is impossible for the lilac bush to withhold its fragrance from anyone. Regardless of who walks by the lilac bush — the preoccupied, the self-absorbed, the unappreciative — the fragrance offers itself to them.

This is how Jesus calls us to be perfect. The Greek word translated as "perfect" in today's gospel is *teleios*. *Teleios* means perfect in the sense of completion or end. It refers to an object's goal or purpose. Thus, for us "to be perfected," means that we *strive* to fulfill the purpose for which we were created — to love God and our neighbor. I emphasize the word *strive* because we all fail in love. But this should not discourage us. As Teresa of Avila once wrote, growth in the spiritual life does not mean that we cease to fall, but that we get up quicker when we do fall.

We can make a million mistakes a day, wear last year's fashions, be overweight, wear socks that don't match, have bad taste in art, be clumsy, sing off key, be politically incorrect, use incorrect grammar, have a superabundance of neurotic tendencies and still be perfect as our heavenly Father is perfect — if our love is indiscriminate.

Second Week of Lent

Sunday

Cycle A: Genesis 12: 1–4

God calls Abraham to leave his native land
and journey to a land unknown.

"[Abraham's] faith erupted him into a way
far-off and strange ... I cry out ... [father Abraham]
come to me in pity. Mine is a far and lonely journey, too" (66). The poet who penned these words,
Sr. Miriam of the Holy Spirit, O.C.D. (Jessica
Powers) lived out her life as a Carmelite nun.
Some may think it strange that a cloistered nun
should find a soul mate in a wandering nomad.
But is it? Do not the strange and unfamiliar paths
that God bids us to walk take different forms? God
called Abraham to leave the land of his kinfolk and
journey to a foreign land, but for many of us faith
bids us to stay where we are. The fifth century hermit Amma Syncletica said, "If you find yourself in
a monastery do not go to another place, for that
will harm you a great deal. Just as the bird who
abandons the eggs she was sitting on prevents
them from hatching, so the monk or the nun grow
cold and their faith dies, when they go from one
place to another" (*The Sayings of the Desert Fathers*
194).

Going forth and staying put are two forms of
faith, for leaving home and staying home each is a

call from God. How many preachers have extolled the faith that gave Abraham the courage to leave home but have never preached a sermon on the faith of a mother who stays home with her children or a child who stays home to take care of an aging parent? And for some, faith's journey takes the form of returning home. We have an example of this in the life of Flannery O'Connor.

In 1950, at the age of twenty-five, Flannery O'Connor began to experience pain and stiffness in her upper body. These were the first symptoms of lupus erythematosus, a debilitating autoimmune disease. At the time she was living with friends in Ridgefield, Connecticut working on her first novel, *Wise Blood,* anticipating success as an author. O'Connor's illness did not stop her from writing, but it did demand that she return to the family farm in Milledgeville, Georgia. She had a deep aversion to returning home, but she accepted the hard reality that her sickness imposed. O'Connor knew that she could not support herself as an author and that she would have to depend upon her mother for care as the disease progressed. O'Connor, a very strong and independent woman, sojourned in the strange and horrifying land of being taken care of by another. It is no coincidence that several of O'Connor's stories center upon a single mother who takes care of a daughter with either a physical or psychological disorder.

O'Connor's choice to return home was as faith-filled as Abraham's choice to leave home.

48   *Second Week of Lent*

Living on a farm in the middle of nowhere iso-lated O'Connor from colleagues and friends. Her chronic illness was another foreign land that she was called forth to wander alone. In a letter to Elizabeth Hester, O'Connor wrote, "I have never been anywhere but sick. In a sense sickness is a place, more instructive than a long trip to Eu-rope, and it's always a place where there's no company, where nobody can follow" (163).

The same is true regarding our journey of faith. Each of us is on a path that no one else can follow, for God calls us to travel along a road uniquely our own.

Sunday

Cycle B: Genesis 22: 1–2, 9, 10–13, 15–18

God commands Abraham to sacrifice his only son Isaac. Abraham's willingness to make this great sacrifice proves his faith in God.

In *The City of God*, dealing specifically with Adam's part in original sin, Augustine wrote, "The man could not bear to be severed from his only companion, even though this involved a partner-ship in sin" (14.11). Centuries later, in *Paradise*

Lost, John Milton expressed Augustine's thought in poetry. Adam says to Eve:

> How can I live without thee, how forgo
> Thy sweet converse and love so dearly
>   joined
> To live again in these wild woods forlorn?
> Should God create another Eve, and I
> Another rib afford, yet loss of thee
> Would never from my heart; no no, I feel
> The link of nature draw me: flesh of flesh,
> Bone of my bone thou art, and from thy
>   state
> Mine never shall be parted, bliss or woe.
> (IX 908–16)

Who cannot empathize with Adam? Who could bear being severed from our greatest love? Who has the capacity to choose to do the will of God that entails sacrificing the greatest gift that we have ever received?

Abraham's sacrifice of Isaac is the story one man's willingness to sacrifice the thing that he loved the most. It is also our story. Each of us is brought to a pass where we must decide whether we are willing to pay the utmost price for our convictions, to obey the dictates of conscience, come what may. Such a crossroads defines who we are, provides a moment of truth that discloses to us the true worth of our mettle. Living in willingness to accept God's will, whatever the cost, is *the* attitude of faith. As Cardinal Newman once prayed, "Grant me, O Merciful Lord, the faith that inspired Abraham to be willing to make whatever sacrifices are necessary to please you." While Abraham's great faith in God and his willingness to sacrifice Isaac is the central theme of this story, we should not overlook that it is also about the purification of faith. How could anyone believe that God could ask Abraham to commit such a monstrous act as to kill his own child?

Abraham was raised in a culture in which human sacrifice was common. Members of his tribe may have even practiced it. Abraham did as God had commanded. He left his kindred and his father's house, but Abraham carried vestiges of his tribal god. It is easy to imagine that Abraham had *thought* God was asking him to sacrifice Isaac, for sometimes when we are willing to do God's will, whatever the price, strange ideas enter our minds. Was this the case with Abraham? If the pagan deities that surrounded Abraham extracted such high price as to sacrifice their own flesh, would not God, who called Abraham to a deeper commitment, ask anything less?

Many of us are like Abraham, sacrificing to a god that is partly pagan. We have an example of this in Maugham's *Of Human Bondage*. Philip Carey, raised by a pious aunt and uncle (a clergyman), is infected by their notion of God. "Philip got up [out of bed] and knelt down to say his prayers. It was a cold morning, and he shivered a little; but he had been taught by his uncle that his prayers were more acceptable to God if he said them in his nightshirt than if he waited till he was dressed. This did not surprise him, for he was beginning to realize that he was the creature of a God who appreciated the discomfort of his worshipers" (39).

The word sacrifice is derived from two Latin words, *sacer* (sacred) and *facere* (to make). God *does* demand sacrifices — not sacrifices that dehumanize us, but sacrifices that sanctify us.

Sunday

Cycle C: Luke 9: 28–36

Jesus is transfigured on Mount Hermon and resolves completely to accept his impending death.

Luke tells us that Jesus was transfigured *while* he was praying. We do not know for certain what he was praying about, but his conversation with Moses and Elijah provides a clue. "They appeared in glory and spoke to him of his departure (Greek *exodus*) which he was about to fulfill in Jerusalem." The *exodus* or departure referred to here is Jesus' death. In Luke's gospel, this is the first time that Jesus had contemplated his death.

Second Week of Lent

On Mount Hermon Jesus made a choice; he resolved to embrace his death fully. At his baptism Jesus accepted his mission as the Suffering Servant of Yahweh, but only now does he confront its stark and gruesome reality. It is one thing to say "yes" to suffering that lies in the far future. Imminent suffering presents a completely different reality. Jesus was changed at the transfiguration because he came to a resolution regarding his own death.

We have all experienced the great release of energy that results when, after years of irresolution, we make an important life decision. We do not realize how much energy living in a perpetual state of avoidance, vacillation, or procrastination consumes until we experience the incredible relief that follows such a decision.

The choice Jesus made at the transfiguration also protected him against any inner vacillation. When Jesus came down the mountain, "He set his face (Greek *sterrizo*) to go to Jerusalem" (Lk 9:51). *Sterrizo* means to make fast, or to fix with an unalterable purpose. Saint Teresa encouraged her sisters to embrace the cross with a "determined determination." In doing so, she wrote, "that person struggles more courageously. He knows that come what may he will not turn back" ("The Way of Perfection" 127).

A definitive choice protects us from inner vacillation. In *The Lord of the Rings* Tolkien portrays this symbolically. At the council of Elrond, a decision has to be made. Someone has to take the One Ring of Power into the evil land of Mordor and cast it into the fire of Mt. Doom. Frodo, who had lived comfortably all of his life, makes a fully conscious choice to be the Ring Bearer. At this point in the story, his uncle Bilbo Baggins gives Frodo a mithril coat.

This coat, as an undergarment made of an extremely strong but light metal, will protect the wearer from many dangers — arrows and the thrusting of spears. Why, asks Jungian analyst Helen Luke, does Bilbo present the mithril coat precisely at the moment that Frodo decides to be the Ring Bearer? What does it symbolize? Luke writes:

> It was at this moment of his complete acceptance of exposure to every kind of danger, without thought of success or failure, that he was given the protection of the mithril coat.... It is not difficult to see the relevance of these things to ourselves. It is surely true that in the life of every person there is one major turning point — a moment of choice when one's basic will (the Frodo in oneself) may say "yes" or "no" to the challenge of one individual way and to the inevitable suffering and danger it involves. It is certain that, if we say "yes" ... then in proportion to the single-mindedness of this decision, we too are given protection.... Every day there is the temptation to go back on our choice ... but each time we decide to take up a respon-

sibility we have sought to evade ... then, in the very moment of our willing self-exposure and conscious acceptance of the task ... we can often literally feel a new invulnerability. (75–76)

Like Jesus, when we decide to embrace the cross with determination, we are transfigured and given courage that protects us against inner vacillation.

Monday

Luke 6: 36–38

Jesus commands us not to judge our neighbor. If we do so, we pass the same judgment upon ourselves.

"Do not judge and you will not be judged. Do not condemn and you will not be condemned." Evaluating is not judging. Sometimes our jobs require us to appraise the behavior of others, be it their work performance, their professional competency, or their physical or emotional capacity to perform some task. Parents must judge which television programs, movies, or acquaintances they allow their children to experience. In a thousand ways, all of us assess and appraise the worth of things. These examples are not the types of judgments that Jesus condemns in today's gospel. Jesus is condemning the judgment we make on a person's culpability or motive. Rash judgments are sinful because in making them we are playing God. Only God knows the motives of the human heart and a person's culpability for his or her actions. Dorotheos of Gaza illustrates these points with a story from the sixth century that, although it contains the limitations of its cultural context, makes an important point.

> I remember once hearing the following story: A slave ship put in at a certain port where there lived a holy virgin who was in earnest about her spiritual life. When she learned about the arrival of the ship she was glad, for she wanted to buy a serving maid for herself. She thought to herself, "I will take her into my home and bring her up in my way of life so that she knows nothing of the evils of this world." [There were two small girls on the ship; the virgin bought one of them. The other girl was bought by a leader of a dancing troupe]. Now take a look at God's mystery; see what his judgment was. Which of us could give any judgment about this case? The holy virgin took one of these little ones to bring her up in the fear of God, to instruct her in every good work. The other unfortunate child ... was trained in the works of the devil. Neither child knew where she had

come from; one is found in the hands of God and the other falls into the hands of the devil. Is it possible to say that what God asks from the one he asks also from the other? Surely not! Suppose they both fell into fornication or some other deadly sin; is it possible that they both face the same judgment or that their fall is the same? How does it appear to the mind of God when one learns about the Judgment and about the Kingdom of God, while the other unfortunate knows nothing of it, never hears anything good but only the contrary, everything shameful...? How can he allow them to be examined by the same standard? (134)

This story contains two truths about rash judgments. First, they are based upon ignorance; we are blind to the forces that have shaped another person's life. Second, even regarding the blatantly sinful *behavior* of our neighbor, we cannot judge the degree of his or her *guilt*.

It is easy to judge our neighbor's guilt rashly, especially if we have never been tempted to commit our neighbor's sin. But not being tempted in an area is not due to any merit of our own but purely to the grace of God. This is true even for souls that are in the state of union with God. Teresa of Avila wrote in this regard: "Nor should it pass through your minds that, since these souls have such determination and strong desires not to commit any imperfection for anything on earth, they fail to commit many imperfections, and even sins. Advertently, no; for the Lord must give souls such as these very particular help against such a thing. I mean venial sins, for from what these souls can understand they are *free* from mortal sins, although they are *not immune* [italics added]" ("The Interior Castle" 444). *But for the grace of God there go I*, is a reality for all of us, no matter how far we have traveled on the spiritual road.

Tuesday

Matthew 23: 1–12

Jesus tells his disciples that because the Pharisees have succeeded Moses as teachers, they should observe what the Pharisees teach but not follow their example.

In today's gospel, Jesus is trying to correct a common *ad hominem* form of blindness. He tells his disciples that even if the Pharisees do not practice what they preach, the truths they teach are still valid. "The scribes and the Pharisees sit on Moses' seat; therefore, do whatever they teach you and follow it; but do not do as they do."

God is not bound to use pure, holy, intelligent, or rational instruments to communicate his truth, beauty, and goodness to us. Some people just cannot comprehend this truth, for they believe that only a pure vessel can communicate the Divine. In Peter Shaffer's play *Amadeus,* Salieri is such a person. He resents it deeply that God had chosen Mozart as the instrument through which heavenly music is born. Salieri says, "It seemed to me that I had heard a voice of God — and that it issued from a creature whose own voice I had also heard — and it was the voice of an obscene child" (29). God often chooses to speak through obscene, worldly, and even wicked conduits. If God is likely to do anything, it is the *unlikely.*

Roman Catholics understand that sacraments operate *ex opere operato,* that is, grace is present in the sacraments *independent of* either the disposition or personal holiness of the priest who administers them. A similar *ex opere operato* principle operates throughout the whole of life.

We may not like the instrument that God chooses to speak the truth to us. In fact, he or she may be our enemy. Furthermore, the enemy who speaks to us may do so with ill intent. For example, an enemy may tell us the truth only to cause us pain. Nevertheless, God may have chosen this enemy as the instrument to communicate his truth to us.

Worldly wisdom tells us to "consider the source." Conversely, however, Saint Thomas tells us that we must consider *what* a person says and not *who* says it. Even if the devil were to speak to us, if he spoke the truth, we should attend to what he says. In a similar vein, Saint Teresa wrote, "Whenever we see the image of our Lord, it is good to pay it reverence, even if the devil had painted it.... For when we see a very good painting, even though we might know that a bad man did it, we shouldn't fail to esteem the image that was painted nor should we pay attention to the painter and therefore lose our devotion" (*The Collected Works of St. Teresa of Avila* 140).

How often do we fail to hear God's message because of our negative feelings toward the messenger?

Wednesday

Matthew 20: 17–28

The mother of James and John asks Jesus to have her sons sit at his left and right hand in his kingdom. The other disciples' resentment at this request occasions Jesus to teach where true greatness lies — in service.

"When the ten heard it, they were angry (Greek *eganaktesan*) with the two brothers." *Eganaktesan* is a strong word, indicating anger and deep resentment. The disciples resented James and John deeply for trying to take unfair advantage of their relationship with Jesus. Also *how* the brothers were jockeying for power fueled the others' resentment. How low can you go — using your own mother? And considering that the apostles were always arguing among themselves about which of them was the greatest, one cannot help but wonder if part of their resentment lay in the fact that they had not thought of using John's and James' ploy themselves.

Today's gospel is about the exercise of power. Jesus condemns power that *lords it over* others but commends power that *influences* the lives of others. Gregory the Great writes that the best form of authority proceeds from the way that we live. "The ruler should be exemplary in his conduct, that by his manner of life he may show the way of life to his subjects, and that the flock, following the teaching and conduct of its shepherd, may proceed the better by example rather than words" (49).

Or as Francis of Assisi once said, "Let us always preach the gospel and sometimes use words." In short, we *lead* others by *following* Christ. We exercise power for the good by the way that we live.

One of Charles Dickens' most endearing characters is Joe Gargery, the kind, gentle, hard- working blacksmith in *Great Expectations.* Pip, an orphan who lives with his shrewish sister and her husband Joe, says of him, "Home had never been a very pleasant place to me, because of my sister's temper, but Joe had sanctified it" (106–07). Is there any authority stronger than that of persons who by their very presence sanctify their surroundings?

Thursday

Luke 16: 19–31

While the rich man (Dives) feasts every day at his table, Lazarus starves to death on Dives' doorstep.

In *A Christmas Carol,* Charles Dickens presents us with an image of hell. As Marley's Ghost departs, Scrooge follows him to the window. "The air was filled with phantoms, wandering hither and thither in restless haste, and moaning as they went. Every one of them wore chains like Marley's Ghost.... He had been quite familiar with one old ghost, in a white waistcoat, with a monstrous iron safe attached to its ankle, who cried piteously at being unable to assist a wretched woman with an infant, whom it saw below, upon a doorstep. The misery with them all was, clearly, *that they sought to interfere, for good, in human matters, and had lost the power for ever* [italics added]" (16). The "great chasm" fixed between Lazarus and Dives is not of God's making. Rather, Dives has lost forever his ability to love — the power to interfere for good in human affairs. How do we lose the capacity to love? Gradually.

Lazarus lay at Dives' gate *every day.* Dives saw Lazarus as he left and entered his house. At times, Dives may have even had to step over him.

There must have been a time when Dives was moved at such a pitiful sight. But the more we are moved to act but choose not to respond, the more we build up a tolerance to the sight of human suffering. And there may come a day when we no longer have the capacity even to be moved.

Psychiatrist R. D. Laing once said that we become blind when we fail to notice that we fail to notice. Such was the case of Dives. Over time, Lazarus became merely a part of the landscape. Lazarus had become invisible, someone whom Dives had walked by so often, that he became an object. People become invisible when we walk by never acknowledging their presence. In this regard, Harvard psychiatrist Robert Coles relates the following experience of one of his students:

> One day Ben told me that he'd just, for the first time, noticed and spoken to a man he passed several times almost every day: the person who checked students as they entered the library (for a proper identification) and as they left it (for what they were carrying out). Why is it, the student asked, that he had no idea who this man was, what he looked like, though he'd seen him daily? Many times the man had spoken to him, he began to realize, yet he had never replied even in brief kind: "I first noticed him, *saw* him, a few days ago. I first *heard* him then, too. The guy ahead of me was checking out.

That man thanked him for opening up his book bag, and smiled at him. He told the guy to have a good day — I guess because the student looked at him." You can acknowledge someone through a look. You can dismiss someone completely by not looking at him. (*The Call of Stories* 70–71)

Each day we have brief encounters with people as Ben had with the man at the library. And like Ben, we can choose either to acknowledge their presence or to ignore them. The danger of passing by people without even acknowledging their existence is that such behavior gradually erodes our capacity to love.

Friday

Genesis 37: 3–4, 12–13, 17–28

Because of their envy, Joseph's brothers sell him into slavery.

Joseph dreamt that while he and his brothers were binding sheaves, his sheaf stood upright suddenly and those of his brothers bowed down to the ground before his. Imprudently, Joseph told his brothers about his dream. They already hated him because he was his father's favorite, and this only

Second Week of Lent

increased their animosity. So when they had their chance they sold Joseph into Egypt, saying with vindictive triumph, "Now we shall see what comes of his dreams."

Ironically, Joseph's dream was fulfilled as a result of his brothers' decision to sell him into slavery. Years later, when the brothers came to Egypt to procure food in time of famine, they had to present themselves to Joseph, who at the time was a high official in the government. And they "bowed down before him to the ground" (Gn 43: 26). Joseph's brothers became instruments of fulfilling the dream they wanted to destroy. In doing so, they also became unwitting players in the drama of salvation history. God's ways are mysterious, and often he uses the evil designs of others to fulfill his plans.

Joseph suffered at the hands of his brothers but eventually realized that their evil deed was the instrument of God's design. Joseph said to his brothers, "And now do not be distressed or angry with yourselves, because you sold me here. God sent me before you to preserve life.... So it was not you who sent me here but God" (Gn 45: 5, 8).

God writes straight with crooked lines in all of our lives. His plan of salvation isn't operative only when things are going well. Often the evil that we suffer from the hands of others becomes the instrument of our redemption and transformation. Like Joseph, however, we usually come to this insight only years after the evil has been inflicted upon us.

We have an example of this in *Great Expectations*. Estella, raised by Miss Havisham to be a cold and heartless woman, is transformed through the cruelty of her husband. She says to Pip at the end of the story, "But you said to me, 'God bless you, God forgive you!' And if you could say that to me then [when I treated you cruelly] you will not hesitate to say that to me now — *now, when suffering has been stronger than all other teaching, and has taught me to understand what your heart used to be. I have been bent and broken, but I hope into a better shape* [italics added]" (451). Or as Pip mused in the original ending of the novel, "I was very glad afterwards to have had the interview, for in her face and in her voice, and in her touch, she gave me the assurance that suffering had been stronger than Miss Havisham's teaching, and had given her a heart to understand what my heart used to be" (453). Suffering is one of the great teachers of life. In Estella's case, cruelty became an instrument that turned her heart of stone into a heart of flesh.

God does not create evil, but he does use it in his plan of salvation. When we suffer evil at the hands of others we participate in the mystery of the Cross.

Saturday

Luke 15: 1–3, 11–32

In the parable of the Prodigal Son, we see a faint image of God's love for us, a love that always beckons us to return home.

In George Herbert's poem "The Pulley," God pours out every blessing upon humankind — beauty, wisdom, honor and pleasure, holding back one gift — *rest*. For God thought to himself, "If I should ... bestow this jewel also on my creature/ He would adore my gifts instead of me/And rest in nature, not in the God of Nature." God's choice to withhold rest from humankind created restlessness and dissatisfaction in the human heart. God uses unrest as the pulley that draws human hearts out of the quicksand of worldly self-absorption back to God.

> Yet let him keep the rest,
> But keep them with repining restlessness:
> Let him be rich and weary, that at least,
> If goodness lead him not, yet weariness
> May toss him to my breast.
> (284)

This stanza contains two truths. The first is that the longing God has planted in our hearts makes us strangers on this earth. Malcolm

Muggeridge considered the feeling of being a stranger in this world one of the greatest blessings that God had ever bestowed upon him. He wrote,

> This sense of being a stranger, which first came to me at the very beginning of life, I have never quite lost, however engulfed I might be ... in earthly pursuits.... For me there has always been — and I count it the greatest of all blessings — a window never finally blackened out, a light never finally extinguished. I had a sense, sometimes enormously vivid, that I was a stranger in a strange land; a visitor, not a native, a displaced person. The feeling, I was surprised to find, gave me a great sense of satisfaction, almost of ecstasy. [When the feeling went away, I asked myself], would it ever return — the lostness? I strain my ears to hear it, like distant music; my eyes to see it, a very bright light very far away. Has it gone forever? And then, Ah! the relief. Like slipping away from a sleeping embrace, silently shutting a door behind one, tiptoeing off in the grey light of dawn — a stranger again. The only ultimate disaster that can befall us, I have come to realize, is to feel ourselves to be at home here on earth. As long as we are aliens, we cannot forget our true homeland. (30–31)

Muggeridge can say, paradoxically, that he felt "connected" to his real self only when he felt a stranger in this world because his longing for a place beyond this world was an experience of his true homeland — heaven.

In the parable of the prodigal son, the Greek phrase translated "coming to his senses at last," literally means "having come to himself." What brought the prodigal son home to himself was his *hunger.* The same is true with us.

"If goodness lead him not, yet *weariness* may toss him to my breast." The second truth that Herbert's poem contains is that God loves us so much that he welcomes his prodigal children back home for any reason whatsoever. God does not demand that our motives be either noble or pure as a prerequisite for being accepted home. The prodigal son came home because he was hungry and tired. It made no difference to his father *why* he came home, as long as he had him home safe and sound. But like the prodigal son, our guilt makes us feel that we no longer even deserve to be called God's children.

Our guilt distorts the merciful countenance of God. Julian of Norwich tells us that when we are submerged in our guilt "We believe that God may be angry with us because of our sins." In consequence, we project our guilt on God as anger and then fear punishment. But when cleansed of our guilt we see clearly. Julian writes, "And then our courteous Lord shows himself to

the soul, happily and with the gladdest countenance, welcoming it as a friend, as if it had been
in pain and in prison saying, 'My dear darling, I
am glad you have come to me in all your woe. I
have *always been with you*' [italics added] and now
you see me loving, and we are made one in bliss"
(246).

The restless longing that God has planted in
our hearts is more than *our* desire for heaven. It is
God's loving invitation for us to return home.

Third Week of Lent

Sunday

Cycle A: John 4:5–42

Jesus speaks to the Samaritan woman at
the well and offers her living water.

In Saint John's deeply symbolic gospel, literal
images point beyond themselves to a deep spiritual
meaning. We have an example of this in today's
gospel. The Samaritan woman said, "Sir ... you
have no bucket and this well (Greek *phrear*) is
deep." Jesus responded, "The water that I will give
will become a spring (Greek *pege*) of water gushing
up to eternal life." *Phrear* refers to a cistern, something man-made; whereas *pege* is a stream that
wells up out of the ground. The former is water ac-
quired by our own efforts; the latter is water that
we receive. In the Bible, water symbolizes various
spiritual realities — chiefly, Divine Life and Wisdom (e.g., "the water of wisdom," Sirach 15:3).
From this perspective, the water obtained from a
phrear represents human wisdom and the water received from a *pege* symbolizes Divine Wisdom.

British psychoanalyst D. W. Winnicott said
that he experienced the most significant turning
point in his professional career on the day that he
no longer felt the need to be clever for his clients.
Once he no longer preoccupied himself with im-
pressing clients with his intellectual acumen, he
was able to tap into a deep well of wisdom that lay

beyond his ego. Released from the self-absorption of trying to formulate a psychologically astute response, he could relax and hear wisdom not of his own making. Jesus said, "The word you hear is not mine, it comes from the Father who sent me" (Jn 14:24). The New English translation renders this verse, "I am not the *source* of my own words." What is the source of my words? From whence do they arise — from my ego or my spirit?

The water that wells up from the deep underground stream of God's life within us is twice-blest. It relieves the parched, weary soul whose ego is forever digging for something that can never satisfy. John of the Cross compares the ego's appetites to "leaking cisterns that cannot contain the water that slakes thirst" (132). When the momentary thrill of having dazzled our neighbor with our worldly wisdom has subsided, we feel empty inside.

Also, when our words and deeds arise from the indwelling fountain of God's presence, our neighbor is the beneficiary. Teresa of Avila writes, "When our active works arise from this interior root [of God's indwelling presence] they become lovely and very fragrant flowers.... And the fragrance from these flowers spreads to the benefit of many. It is a fragrance that lasts, not passing quickly, but having great effect" ("Meditations on the Song of Songs" 256).

Can I detach myself from the need to impress others with my knowledge or cleverness in order to hear the Divine Wisdom dwelling in my heart?

Sunday

Cycle B: Exodus 20: 1–17

On Mount Sinai God gives Moses the Ten
Commandments.

"I, the Lord, your God, am a jealous God,
punishing children for the iniquity of parents, to
the third and fourth generation...." Taken literally, this verse says that God punishes people for
what their ancestors have done. Even though this
interpretation does not coincide with our belief
in a just and loving God, this verse contains an
inexorable truth that may be summed up in the
old saying, "The apple does not fall far from the
tree." For good or for ill, we have a profound impact upon our children and those entrusted to
our care. Parents cannot protect their child from
their wounded, broken selves, no matter how
holy they may be. We have an example of this in
the life of Saint Thérèse.

Thérèse suffered from scrupulosity all of her
life. She received this trait from her mother Zélie,
also raïsed by a very scrupulous mother. Zélie
was so holy and loving that the Church has declared her Venerable, the first step in becoming a
canonized saint. Nevertheless, she could not prevent passing on this negative trait to her daughter. This is part of the tragedy of original sin; we

pass down to the third and fourth generation wounds and sins of our ancestors.

In the Old Testament, when Ahab repented of his corruption as a ruler, God said to the prophet Elijah, "Have you seen that Ahab has humbled himself before me? Because he has humbled himself before me, I will not bring the disaster in his days; but in his son's days" (1 Kgs 21:29). This sounds unjust, but it is simply an expression of stark reality. Repentance, no matter how sincere, does not have the power to trammel up the consequences of our past actions. Ahab's corrupt reign had infected the whole moral and political fabric of his country. Being sorry for what he had done could not change this. With his father's throne the son also inherited the ill consequences of his reign.

T.S. Eliot wrote that one of the great sufferings of growing older is "the awareness of things ill done and done to others' harm" ("Little Gidding" 54). To realize that we have harmed the people we love the most is the greatest of all sufferings. At such moments, we need to call out for God's mercy and take comfort in the words of Jesus upon the cross, "Father forgive them, for they know not what they do."

Sunday

Cycle C: Luke 13: 1–9

The parable of the fig tree exhorts us not to
live a fruitless life.

In 1970, during a protest at Kent State University, national guardsmen shot and killed several students. Shortly afterwards, psychologists interviewed parents of college-age children. Among other questions, they asked whether the students who had been killed were campus radicals or innocent bystanders. Overwhelmingly, the parents believed that the slain students were campus radicals. Applying to their findings Attribution Theory, which tries to explain how and why people make sense of their world, the psychologists concluded that the majority of parents held that the slain students were radicals because it was too frightening for them to believe otherwise. If they believed that the slain students were innocent bystanders, then they would have to admit that in a similar situation their own children were vulnerable. Whenever disaster strikes, we tend to attribute it to a cause that will protect us from a similar disaster.

This is what the people in today's gospel were trying to do. They had to believe that those killed by Pilate or the falling Tower of Siloam were sinners. This belief protected them from living in an unpredictable world. They were reasoning thus: "All we need to do in order to be safe is to keep the Law, for bad things don't happen to good people." Jesus challenges their thinking by telling them the Parable of the Fig Tree, which teaches that to avert spiritual disaster it is not enough to keep the Law. Our lives must bear fruit.

The Greek word translated "wasting (*katargeo*) the soil," means unused, idle, inactive, or useless. From a spiritual perspective, our life is useless and barren, if, like the fig tree, we provide shade only for our selves and offer no nourishment to others.

The parable is consoling, for it proclaims a season of grace, a second chance, a stay of execution. Each day when we wake up, we are given another opportunity to truly live life by loving our neighbor. But the parable is also sobering, for it warns us that our opportunities are not endless. Thoreau wrote that he wanted to live deliberately in order to avoid the ultimate disaster of life, that at the moment of death he would "discover that [he] had not lived" (86). This is what we must fear.

Monday

2 Kings 5: 1–15

The army commander Naaman is cured of
his leprosy when, at Elisha's command, he
bathes seven times in the Jordan River.

Harvard psychiatrist Robert Coles writes of
the time he first met Dorothy Day.

> She was sitting at a table, talking with a
> woman who was ... quite drunk, yet deter-
> mined to carry on a conversation.... I found
> myself increasingly confused by what
> seemed to be an interminable, essentially
> absurd exchange ... between two middle-
> aged women — the alcoholic ranting and
> the silent nodding [of Dorothy Day]. Fi-
> nally silence fell upon the room. Dorothy
> Day asked the woman if she would mind
> an interruption. She got up and came over
> to me. She said, "Are you waiting to talk
> with one of us?" *One of us*: with those three
> words she had cut through layers of self-
> importance, a lifetime of bourgeois privi-
> lege, and scraped the hard bone of pride....
> With those three words, so quietly and po-
> litely spoken, she had indirectly told me
> what the Catholic Worker Movement is all

about and what she herself was like. (*Dorothy Day: A Radical Devotion* xviii)

Naaman, a "highly esteemed and respected" man of rank, was accustomed to a life of privilege. Like many people in authority, he was used to people doing his bidding. It is no wonder, therefore, that he was incensed with Elisha. Naaman drove up to Elisha's house in his Cadillac and parked it out front. He stayed in his car because he *expected* Elisha to come out to him. Naaman imagined that all he had to do was roll down his window so that Elisha could say a few prayers over him and then he could drive off.

Naaman was a leper. But he needed to be cured of something far worse than a skin disease. As a man of power and privilege, he had become infected with the same disease that Dickens writes of in *A Tale of Two Cities.* Dickens describes the aristocracy of the French court as being disfigured by "the leprosy of unreality" (111). Pampered by their life of privilege, they could not suffer any delay or inconvenience. None of us may be aristocrats; nevertheless, we can be clothed with the leprosy of self-importance and bourgeois privilege. How often do we get angry or incensed when we are not attended to immediately?

Tuesday

Matthew 18: 21–35

Our capacity to receive God's forgiveness is conditioned by our willingness to forgive one another.

We tend to be very compassionate and understanding toward the faults, failings, and sins of others at two moments in life. The first is when we are overwhelmed by guilt. Our desire that someone relieve our burden of guilt makes us compassionate toward those carrying the same burden. The second moment is immediately after confession. The utter relief at shedding our burden of guilt makes us want to share the same joy with fellow sinners.

The master condemned the unmerciful servant severely because the servant hardened his heart at the very moment that it had been softened. The unmerciful servant sinned not only by mistreating his fellow servant but also by dismissing the joy of being forgiven. He received the blessing of being pitied but refused to extend that same blessing to his brother. He was released from his prison of guilt but on the way out, shut the gates of mercy on his fellow human beings. Mercy is rooted in recognizing our common bond with our neighbor. If we cannot extend mercy at the very moment when we are experiencing that bond, can we ever be merciful?

The master retracted his mercy from his servant. This action symbolizes the truth that mercy cannot survive in a merciless heart. Any blessing that we receive but refuse to extend to others will wither within us. The fruit of being forgiven is not the feeling of relief that proceeds from receiving forgiveness. That is simply the immediate *effect* of being forgiven. The fruit of being forgiven is an invitation to become a merciful person.

Just as mercy is twice-blest, blessing the one who gives and blessing the one who takes, a lack of mercy is twice-cursed. The unmerciful inflict suffering on their victims and punishment upon themselves. This is what the harsh ending of today's gospel means. "Then in anger the master handed him over to the torturers.... My heavenly Father will treat you in exactly the same way unless each of you forgives his brother or sister from his heart." God does not dispense *quid pro quo.* Rather, it reflects the unavoidable reality that mercy cannot enter into a merciless heart.

Wednesday

Deuteronomy 4: 1, 5–9

Moses exhorts the Israelites to remember
the great deeds that the Lord has done for
them and to not let those deeds slip from
their memories.

Upon recovering from a long illness, Wilfred
Sheed reflected:

> The spiritual life becomes very simple when
> you're sick. You pray to get better, and if
> and when you do, you don't need to be told
> to be grateful about it: it gushes out of you.
> And you discover, in the same giddy rush,
> that just being alive ... is astoundingly good.
> G. K. Chesterton once said that if a person
> were to fall into the waters of forgetfulness
> and come out on the other side, he would
> think he had arrived in paradise. But all you
> need to do is to spend a couple of months on
> your back, or return home from a war and
> come downstairs to have breakfast in your
> own house. So my private proofs of God ...
> begin with this: the sheer capacity for happi-
> ness, and one's sense, when it happens, that
> this is correct and normal and not some
> freak of nature. When health returns, it

feels like coming home ... and the other thing, the bad news — the broken leg or even the mental breakdown — feels like the freak. But now you are back to where you belong, in harmony with the universe. And from this I deduce with some conviction that the universe is *essentially* a good place to be, despite appearances. (10)

We feel gratitude most poignantly shortly after we have recovered from a great sickness or immediately after unburdening ourselves of some mental anguish. We feel deep relief because we still *remember* our pain. But as time passes and we get further and further away from that initial experience of relief, our sense of gratitude fades because we *forget* how bad it really was.

This is what happened to the Hebrews. When they were in slavery, they cried out to God to be released. And when Moses brought them out of their bondage, they were grateful, but only for a while. As they sojourned in the desert, year in and year out, their memory of what God had done for them began to fade. And whenever anything went wrong, they complained to Moses. "Why did you bring us out into this desert? We were better off back in Egypt!" Past pain is no match for present suffering. We forget how bad we had it.

Thus, Moses exhorts the Hebrews: "Take care and watch yourselves closely, so as neither to forget the things that your own eyes have seen, nor let them slip from your mind as long as you

Third Week of Lent

live...." Forgetting the things of the past does not mean the inability to recall an event. Rather, it means that a past event ceases to have an impact upon the present. Remembrance is an act of *re-membering* ourselves, to reconnect ourselves to the great graces that we have received.

God's saving mercy has brought all of us through difficult times. We should not let what God has done for us slip from our memory. We need to remember the pain of the past. Doing so fosters gratitude and helps us keep the little annoyances of daily life in perspective.

Thursday

Luke 11:14–23

Jesus casts out a demon and is accused of being in cahoots with the devil.

What choice do we have if people we hate have done something praiseworthy? Well, we can do the decent thing and pay them a compliment. Or we can discredit their deed either by calling their motive into question or by insinuating that they performed this deed by evil means. We see the latter happening to Jesus in today's gospel. The bystanders could not repudiate Jesus' good deed in casting out the mute spirit, so they accused him of doing so with diabolical assistance. Jesus does not deny the allegation. He knows that to do so would be futile. He simply asks his detractors a question. "If I cast out devils by Beelzebul, by whom do your people cast them out?"

Jesus' question forces them to examine a basic contradiction that operates in all of our lives, a specific form of blindness that we commonly call a double standard. All of us have people in our lives who either can do no wrong or do no right. We canonize some people but demonize others. How does such a process begin?

Psychologists speak of the halo effect and the devil effect. The halo effect consists of our having an overall positive impression about someone based upon a single characteristic. For example, psychological studies have found that we frequently generalize social and intellectual qualities from physical beauty. In short, when we find a person physically attractive, we presume that he or she is intelligent or competent.

The devil effect works the opposite of the halo effect. It happens when we generalize from one negative trait to a person's entire personality. Thus, we may consider a disheveled person ignorant, uncultured, or uncouth based upon his or her appearance. The halo effect and the devil effect are classic examples of judging a book by its cover.

Such judgments say little about our neighbor but speak volumes about ourselves. For example, if we roll our eyes at a person who isn't "cultured enough" to know which fork to use when eating salad, are we not revealing our own superficiality? To overreact to such a trivial *faux pas* reveals our own pettiness. The people in our lives that we tend to demonize are often angels in disguise who bear a message of self-knowledge that we need to hear.

Friday

Hosea 14: 2–10

The prophet Hosea calls the Israelites to return to God and forsake the idols of their own making.

"We shall say no more, 'Our God,' to the work of our hands." People don't worship work. Rather, they offer their life's blood for what work affords, be it power, prestige, or possessions. The pagan cults that worship power, prestige or possessions are rooted in fear. Power provides a reassurance against helplessness; prestige offers protection against humiliation, and possessions assuage the fear of destitution.[2] But each god betrays its worshipers. For the more we dedicate our lives to protecting ourselves against insecurity, the more insecure we feel.

The story of the king who had a nightmare reveals a deep truth about insecurity. He called in his wizard to interpret his dream. The wizard told the king that the dream predicted he would be murdered on his next birthday and all of his possessions stolen. Out of fear, the king stockpiled his riches in his throne room and ordered guards to surround it. The closer his birthday drew, the more afraid he became. He moved his riches to a smaller room with fewer entranceways and placed his most trusted guards around it. On the eve of his birthday, he ordered that all of his riches be piled in a vault. The king sat inside the vault and ordered its only entrance sealed up with bricks, to be torn down a minute after midnight, the day after his birthday. When they tore the wall down, his men found the king dead. He had suffocated. His dream came true. He was murdered, and his possessions were taken from him. The culprit was his own fear.

Our deep insecurities are insatiable. We will never feel completely secure. The more we placate our fears the stronger they become. We cannot defeat them, nor should we try. The king did not have the power to stop feeling afraid; his dream was too frightening. But he did have the ability to not give into his fear. The same is true with us.

Saturday

Luke 18: 9–14

In the parable of the publican and the Pharisee, Jesus teaches that the basis of true prayer is humility.

The Pharisee in today's gospel is no hypocrite. Everything that he says is true. He isn't crooked, adulterous or grasping. He does fasts twice a week and pays tithes on everything he owns. The Pharisee used his undeniably admirable behavior as a means of self-aggrandizement. This was his fatal sin. He was so engrossed in gazing into the mirror at his moral rectitude and posturing before the world as a paragon of virtue, that he did not realize that he was not even praying. Rather, he was giving God a progress report on his spiritual advancement. How do we gauge our spiritual growth?

Pop psychology promotes the myth that feeling good about oneself is a sign of health. Today's gospel challenges this presupposition. The Pharisee felt good about himself but was blind to his spiritual condition; whereas, the tax collector felt wretched about himself but was facing the truth about his life. How we feel about ourselves is not a reliable barometer of our spiritual lives. A better gauge of our spiritual health is how we look upon our neighbor.

The Pharisee, dressed in regal haughtiness, looked down upon the tax collector as his moral inferior. In the spirit of Uriah Heep, he "umbly" thanked God that he was not like the rest of men. Again, the Pharisee is speaking the truth, for superciliousness renders a person ridiculous. It transforms him or her into an inveterate bore.

Editor Frank Harris, a good friend of Oscar Wilde, constantly boasted of his social contacts and all the grand houses in which he had stayed. One night at a party, Harris rambled on and on about his social engagements. Wilde, who had reached his limit of boredom, interjected, "Yes, dear Frank, we believe you have dined in every house in London — *once*."

John Climacus writes, "God has arranged that no one can see his own faults as clearly as his neighbor does" (226). Seeing the pained look of boredom in the faces of our neighbors as we drone on about ourselves, perhaps would shame us into humility.

Fourth Week of Lent

Sunday

Cycle A: John 9: 1–41

Jesus restores sight to a man blind from birth by rubbing spittle on his eyes. The man is expelled from the synagogue because he believes that Jesus is the Messiah.

Jesus tells us that the man's blindness was not the result of sin but had a purpose — that "God's works might be revealed in him." In short, it provided the context in which God's healing grace could be manifested. But being healed is not synonymous with being cured. Psychiatrist Viktor Frankl relates the following incident:

> A nurse in my department suffered from a tumor which proved to be inoperable. In her despair the nurse asked me to visit her. Our conversation revealed that the cause of her despair was not so much the illness in itself as her incapacity to work. She had loved her profession ... and now she could no longer follow it.... I tried to explain to her that to work eight or ten hours per day is not a great thing.... But to be eager to work and be incapable to work, yet not despair would be an achievement few could attain. And then I asked her: "Are you not being unfair to all those thousands of sick people to whom you

have dedicated your life; are you not being unfair to act now as if the life of an incurable invalid were without meaning? If you behave as if the meaning of your life consisted in being able to work so many hours a day, you take away from all sick people the right to live and the justification for their existence." (*The Doctor and The Soul* xii)

The nurse's terminal illness provided the context of a healing. She was healed of identifying the meaning of her life with her work. Also, her acceptance of her illness became a source of strength and meaning to others.

Any sickness, disease, physical deformity, or abnormality, even a minor suffering like a headache, can serve a divine purpose. One day, Sr. Marie of the Trinity, a novice of Saint Thérèse, was crying. Thérèse told her that she should try to accustom herself to not showing her little sufferings. For, "Nothing contributed so much to making community life depressing as emotional ups and downs" (*St. Thérèse of Lisieux: By Those Who Knew Her* 244). When we make a big deal out of our small sufferings we can become a burden to others.

Thérèse's admonition to suffer in silence is sage advice. The less we inflict our ailments upon others, the more we are healed of our tendency to complain about them. Also, our choice to suffer in silence shows forth the work of God. Is there any greater work of God than charity?

Sunday

Cycle B: John 3: 14–21

Jesus tells Nicodemus that just as the
bronze serpent was an instrument of healing, so too will the Son of Man be the
source of salvation when he is lifted up on
the Cross.

"Just as Moses lifted up the serpent in the wilderness, so must the Son of Man be lifted up,
that whoever believes in him may have eternal
life." This image refers to the time that God sent
Seraph serpents among the people as a punishment for their complaints against God and
Moses. Those who were bitten but still lived
begged Moses to intercede for them. God told
Moses to make a bronze serpent and mount it on
a pole. "And everyone who is bitten shall look at
it and live" (Nm 21: 9). Why would looking
upon the bronze serpent bring healing? Because
it symbolizes acknowledging the consequences of
one's actions. It means looking upon what we
have done to ourselves and to others. This is the
first step in healing. The serpent mounted on the
pole is a symbol of Jesus upon the cross. On the
cross we see what our sins have done. We have
killed Beauty, Truth, and Goodness. As we grow
older, the cross is set before our eyes more and

more as our sinful past looms up before us and we see the damage that lies in the wake of our lives.

But more than an icon of our sins, the Cross is *the* manifestation of God's infinite mercy. It is God's promise that the final judgment upon our lives is mercy and forgiveness. "Christ's death on the cross is a judgment of judgment," Maximus the Confessor puts it (Clément 49). How can this be otherwise? Jesus, who allowed himself to be murdered, offered his murderers forgiveness as he hung dying. In the Cross God reveals completely unmerited forgiveness.

If, when we look upon the Cross, we see only our sins, we are not looking deeply enough. Sin, which is an offense against God, cannot be separated from God's forgiveness. Such a myopic way of looking at sin can result in what Saint Teresa considers one of the great dangers of the spiritual life — discouragement. If we look at our sins isolated from God's mercy, we do not perceive them correctly. Teresa tells us that we should look at our sins against the backdrop of God's mercy, as if we were looking at a black dot against a white background. Excessive introspection upon one's sinfulness is dangerous because we see only the black dot. "Just as Moses lifted up the serpent in the wilderness, so must the Son of Man be lifted up, that whoever *believes* in him may have eternal life." The belief that Jesus is referring to is *trust in God's mercy.*

Sunday

Cycle C: Luke 15: 1–3, 11–32

In the parable of the prodigal son a man loses both of his sons — the first through self-indulgence, the second through self-righteousness.

The Parable of the Prodigal Son leaves us with an unanswered question: Does the elder son join in the celebration of his brother's return or does he stay outside fuming in his self-righteousness? The door is unbarred. He can go in whenever he chooses. Only his inability to enter into his father's joy keeps him outside.

Within this perspective we can understand Jesus' words: "If you forgive the faults of others, your heavenly Father will forgive you yours. If you do not forgive others, neither will your Father forgive you." If we misinterpret these words, we can conclude erroneously that God withholds forgiveness from us when we withhold it from others. In reality, when we do not forgive others, we lose the capacity to receive the forgiveness that God offers us.

Jesus condemns not the elder son, but his self-righteousness. Self-righteousness can cloak itself in many forms, even the guise of humility. Even the prodigal son himself has a peculiar self-righteousness that declares, "I may have my faults and failings; I may have even done wicked things in my life, but at least I'm not self-righteous like my brother." Such a disclaimer not only proclaims one's moral superiority but also can even contain a sort of boast. It's the pride of the initiated sophisticate who smiles down with condescension upon his inexperienced brother. "What does my brother know of life? He's never been off my father's farm. He's never been in the big city. My God, he's never even disobeyed one of my father's orders." Tolkien labels such an attitude "inverted hypocrisy." He held that while we are somewhat free from the common form of hypocrisy that professes a holier than thou attitude, we are subject to an inverted form of hypocrisy that consists of "professing to be worse than we are" (337).

The two brothers in today's gospel may resemble each other more than either of them would care to admit. Rigid, overly moralistic, self-righteous people are vulnerable to abandoning themselves to a self-indulgent, hedonistic lifestyle. Conversely, hedonistic individuals are often blind to the self-righteousness that they project upon others.

Monday

John 4: 43–54

Jesus returns home to Capernaum and restores to health the son of a royal official.

All of us have had bad days. Some of them are bad because of circumstances beyond our control — a traffic jam that makes us miss our flight or rain that cancels a long-awaited day at the beach. But sometimes a day goes bad because we have made it so. For example, if we begin a day in a foul mood, our ill temper will seep out through our behavior. We will be impatient, even nasty with family, friends, and colleagues. And if a recipient of our animus tells us where we can go, we blow up and storm off in a huff, telling ourselves that we are surrounded by jerks. This only deepens our foul mood.

The sinlessness of Jesus did not prevent him from having a bad day, even a bad day of his own making. In today's gospel, Jesus seems to be in a foul mood. He lashes out at the man who begs him to cure his son: "Unless you see signs and wonders, you will not believe." To understand this harsh remark we must know its context.

Jesus had just arrived home to Galilee from Jerusalem. He was tired from a long trip and perhaps afraid, for we are told that Jesus fled Jerusalem because his success in curing many people had incurred the hatred of the religious leaders (Every time Jesus goes to Jerusalem, his presence creates an open breach with the authorities, such as when he cured the cripple by the pool at Bethesda, forgave the woman caught in adultery, gave sight to the man born blind, and raised Lazarus from the dead — Jn 5:1–47, 7:14–10:21, 11:17–53).

Having recently been rejected by the religious authorities in Jerusalem, Jesus may have anticipated a similar reception when he arrived home. Jesus himself had testified, "No one esteems a prophet in his own country." But Jesus was wrong, for "the people there welcomed him." But they welcomed him for the wrong reason. "They themselves had been at the feast and had seen all that he had done in Jerusalem on that occasion." This is what Jesus feared the most, namely, that the people would only regard him as a wonder-worker.

Within the context of the welter of emotions that Jesus must have felt when he arrived home (e.g., being tired, afraid, expecting to be rejected, being regarded as just a miracle worker) we can understand Jesus' harsh reaction to the man who pleaded for his son's life. The man *wasn't* asking Jesus for a sign, but Jesus read this into the man's motive.

We all have experienced how difficult it is to hear what people are really saying when we are wrapped up in our feelings. This may have been the case with Jesus. But once Jesus was able to hear the man's heartfelt plea, he granted his request. And I suspect that Jesus apologized to the man for having lost his temper.

Like Jesus, all of us have bad days. When we are on edge, we often bite people's heads off. This is part of the human condition. But what do we do when we calm down? After we *react,* do we *respond*?

Tuesday

John 5: 1–16
_____

At the pool of Bethseda, Jesus cures a lame man.
_____

Thornton Wilder sets his play *The Angel that Troubled the Waters* at the Sheep Pool of today's gospel. It opens with the blind, the sick, the lame, and the deformed lying on the ground around the Sheep Pool, waiting for an angel to stir the waters. Unexpectedly, a local physician comes to the pool to be healed. He has come seeking a cure not of a physical ailment but an emotional and moral sickness. He prays to God: "Come, long-expected love. Let the sacred finger and sacred breath stir up the pool.... Free me from this old burden.... Renewal, release me; let me begin again without this fault that bears me down." Suddenly, the Angel of the Pool appears to the physician and says that healing will not be granted to him, for God has a reason why his thorn in the flesh must not be removed. The angel says, "Without your wound where would your power be? It is your very remorse that makes your low voice tremble into the hearts of men. The very angels themselves cannot persuade the wretched and blundering children on earth as can one human being broken on the wheels of living. In Love's service only the wounded soldiers can serve" (146–48).

It is a great mystery why God heals some people and not others. Only a few of the people who came to sit at the Sheep Pool in today's gospel were cured. And those who were cured often had to wait a lifetime. No one can explain why some people go home from Lourdes restored to health and others do not. It is a great mystery shrouded in the silence of Divine Providence. Sometimes God does not heal our ailments so we can minister more effectively to others, as was the case with the man in Wilder's story. At other times, God chooses not to heal us because suffering will prove to be the instrument of our sanctification.

Human suffering can evoke compassion, but in certain circumstances it can produce competition, rivalry, and animosity. The situation at the Sheep Pool is a case in point. After the waters had been stirred, everyone made a mad rush to get into the pool first, for it was believed that only the first person to plunge into the water would be healed. An invisible sign hanging over the portico of the Sheep Pool read, "It's every man for himself."

The man cured in today's gospel told Jesus that he had sat by the pool for thirty-eight years because he had no one to plunge him into the pool once the waters had been stirred. Over the course of the years, in their rush to be healed many may have trampled him. Such people lost a golden opportunity to receive the greatest healing that God could have bestowed — the healing of selfishness. "After you sir, you were here before I was." "Excuse me madam, may I help you? You look like you need some assistance." Such courteous and helpful people may never be cured of their physical ailments, but what of it? In the Kingdom of God, the first shall be last and the last shall be first.

Wednesday

Isaiah 49: 8–15

The prophet Isaiah proclaims a new exodus to God's people — leave Babylon and return to the Promised Land.

After storming the Bastille, the revolutionaries flung its doors open and set the prisoners free. However, some of the newly-freed walked sheepishly up to the prison's entrance, peered outside nervously, and returned to their cells. One reason for this odd behavior was confusion. Another was fear. Many of the inmates had been imprisoned for so long that the outside world had become strange and frightening.

The Jews released from their captivity in Babylon and told that they could go home to Israel resemble the frightened inmates of the Bastille. Many had become so inured to their captivity that the prophet had to prod them to leave. "In a time of favor I answered you ... saying to the prisoners, 'Come out,' to those in darkness, 'Show yourselves.' "

The Babylonian exile lasted fifty years. Most of the Jews who "returned" to Palestine had never been there. They were born and bred in Babylon. They grew up, married, had children and grandchildren in Babylon. Going "home" to Palestine was leaving the only home that they had ever known. After a lifetime of putting down roots in Babylon, many of the Jews resisted breaking camp and relocating. Their situation symbolizes our lives.

All of us have a strong urge to maintain the familiar. For example, when two people get married, both partners instinctively try to re-establish the home of their childhood. This explains why spouses often fight bitterly over trivial issues.

To move outside the familiar is difficult. But sometimes God asks us to do so for our own good.

Today's first reading contains the good news that like a gentle shepherd God leads us beyond our fears. "For he who has pity on them will lead them, and by streams of water will guide them." God truly understands our resistance to change and its accompanying fears. God does not chide us for being human. But he loves us too much let us stay where we are.

Thursday

John 5: 31–47

Jesus tells the Jewish authorities that their inability to believe in him is rooted in their need to accept praise from one another.

In his movie *Zelig,* Woody Allen plays Leonard Zelig, a human chameleon. Because he fears rejection and needs acceptance, Zelig becomes like the people who surround him. In the presence of African Americans, his skin darkens; in an Irish pub he begins to talk about the potato famine and leprechauns; with his therapist he assumes the persona of a psychiatrist.

Zelig is humorous but poignant, for it deals with the human fear of being an outsider and its corresponding need to fit in. Zelig symbolizes the extremes we can go to in order to protect ourselves from disapproval. In the process of becoming *like* others in order to *be liked* by them, Zelig lost his individuality.

C. S. Lewis, in his address "The Inner Ring," described one of the most powerful forces in our lives — the desire to be an "insider" and the fear of being an "outsider." Lewis contends that even if the particular ring that we want to belong to is good in itself, the *desire* to belong can be dangerous because we can gradually compromise our integrity.

Lewis describes this imperceptible process in *The Screwtape Letters*. Screwtape writes to his nephew Wormwood, regarding his "patient" who has just become a member of an inner ring of cynical friends who mock virtue and anything religious. "My Dear Wormwood ... Did he commit himself deeply? I don't mean in words. There is a subtle play of looks and tones and laughs by which a mortal can imply that he is of the same party as those to whom he is speaking. That is the kind of betrayal you should especially encourage, because the man does not fully realize it himself; and by the time he does you will have made withdrawal difficult.... As long as the postponement lasts he will be in a false position. He will be silent when he ought to speak and laugh when he ought to be silent. He will assume, at first only by his manner, but presently by his words, all sorts of cynical and skeptical attitudes which are not really his. But if you play him well, they may become his. All mortals tend to turn into the thing they are pretending to be" (46). Often, this is the price we pay for being a member of an inner ring in good standing.

The words of Jesus in today's gospel "How can you believe, when you accept glory from one another," speak of an inner ring, "an old boys' club" among the clergy of the day. Many of them found it difficult to speak their minds because they feared finding themselves on the outside. John's gospel later states, "Nevertheless many, even of the authorities believed in [Jesus]. But because of the Pharisees they did not confess it, for fear that they would be put out of the synagogue; for they loved human glory more than the glory that comes from God" (Jn 12: 42–3).

Today's gospel calls us to reflect upon these basic questions in life: Whose good opinion are we trying to foster, and whose disapproval do we fear the most? What price are we willing to pay for both?

Friday

Wisdom 2: 1, 12–22

People who follow God's will are often persecuted because others find them a living reproof.

"He became to us a reproof to our thoughts; the very sight of him is a burden to us, because his manner of life is unlike that of others." Thomas More, in Robert Bolt's play *A Man for All Seasons*, is such a person. When everyone else in England accepted the legitimacy of Henry VIII's marriage to Anne Boleyn, More remained silent on the issue. But because More was an honest man, his silence afflicted Henry's conscience. As Cromwell said, "While More's alive the King's conscience breaks into fresh stinking flowers every time he gets up from bed" (79). More's silent witness so pierced Henry's conscience that he cannot live with himself. Only two things could bring Henry peace. "[The King] wants either Sir Thomas More to bless his marriage or Sir Thomas More destroyed" (69).

Because More's silence mirrored Henry's guilty conscience, the king desperately wanted More to bless his marriage. How often do we find ourselves in Henry's situation? We are doing something that we don't feel right about, but we don't want to change our behavior. So we go to someone in order to "discern" what we should do, hoping that he will tell us what we want to hear. The last thing we want is for that person to say, "Well, what do you think God is asking you to do?" Or, "What is your conscience telling you to do?"

Simply living our calling in life as best we can may place us in More's situation. Saint Teresa wrote of such circumstances among her nuns. "There is an outcry by persons a Sister is dealing with.... 'She's trying to make out she's a saint.... There are other better Christians who don't put on all this outward show.' And it's worth noting that she is not putting on any outward show but just striving to fulfill well her state in life. Those she considered her friends turn away from her, and they are the ones who take the largest and most painful bite at her" ("The Interior Castle" 360).

Teresa is describing a familiar situation. A person faithfully doing his or her duty threatens slackers, who then go on the attack. "What are you trying to do, make the rest of us look bad?" "Well, if it isn't little miss brown nose, sucking up to the boss again." To paraphrase Saint Teresa, "She isn't sucking up to anyone; she is only doing her duty."

If we are trying to live the life that God has called us to live, we must accept the fact that we will censure the thoughts of certain people, who will feel hardship merely seeing us. This is what it means to be a prophet.

Saturday

John 7: 40–53

People debate whether Jesus is the Messiah, while the Sanhedrin denounce Jesus without a trial. But there is one dissenting voice — Nicodemus.

What we know about Nicodemus is part fact, part conjecture. We are told that he was a teacher in Israel, which means that he was a prominent member of the Sanhedrin. We are also told that he came to Jesus at night. But *why* he came at night, we don't know. Some assume that he was afraid. This is a reasonable conjecture, considering the hostility of the Sanhedrin toward Jesus. Some have even surmised that Nicodemus was an old man, based upon his question to Jesus, "How can a man be born again after having grown old?" (Jn 3: 4). Nicodemus also may have been a man of means, considering the substantial financial outlay he provided for Jesus' burial.

Assuming that all the above is true, Nicodemus finds himself in a difficult situation. He and other members of the Sanhedrin believed in Jesus (Jn 3: 2) but "did not confess [their belief] for fear that [they] would be put out of the synagogue" (Jn 12: 42–3). One can understand his fear. Nicodemus, an old man, has been a teacher all of his life. If he were ejected from the synagogue, what would he do? How would he support himself? Nevertheless, Nicodemus spoke up in Jesus' defense. "Our law does not judge people without first giving them a hearing to find out what they are doing, does it?"

Some argue that by objecting to the Sanhedrin Nicodemus provided only a timid, half-hearted defense of Jesus. They reason that Nicodemus never disclosed that he believed Jesus to be a teacher sent by God. He never "witnessed" to Jesus. But considering his fear of being expelled from the synagogue, which would entail the loss of his job, Nicodemus showed great courage in raising the objection.

Or maybe Nicodemus wasn't afraid to speak his mind. Maybe he was just very pragmatic. He knew that those opposed to Jesus would not listen to any defense of Jesus, so he made them conscious of their contradictory position. He said to those condemning Jesus for disobeying the Law, that they themselves were violating the Law by condemning Jesus without a fair hearing.

What Nicodemus said didn't seem to make any difference, but we will never know. C. S. Lewis wrote, "[In] disagreements ... the right side may be defeated. That matters very much less than I used to think. The very man who has argued you down will sometimes be found years later, to have been influenced by what you said" (*Reflections on the Psalms* 73).

After the Sanhedrin adjourned, "Each went off to his own house." This may have been the time when Nicodemus's words began to germinate. When we are alone with our thoughts and released from the fear of what other people think, we are able to admit to ourselves what we really believe.

Fourth Week of Lent

Fifth Week of Lent

Sunday

Cycle A: John 11: 1–45

Jesus proclaims that he is the resurrection and the life and raises Lazarus from the dead.

One of the great challenges for any priest is preaching at wakes and funerals. How does one proclaim the Good News of the Resurrection to people crushed with grief, without it sounding like a pious platitude? How does one speak of the immortality of the soul and simultaneously honor another's grief? Our hope in *future* resurrection is no match for *present* grief. In the Preface for Christian Death we read, "The sadness of death *gives way* to the bright promise of immortality." Yes, but it does so grudgingly.

In *A Grief Observed*, C. S. Lewis reflects upon his experience of loss after his wife's death. He writes, "Talk to me about the truth of religion and I'll listen gladly. Talk to me about the duty of religion and I'll listen submissively. But don't come to me about the consolations of religion or I shall suspect that you don't understand" (28).

In today's gospel, Martha gives voice to the consolation of faith: "I know he will rise again ... in the resurrection on the last day." But she prefaces her belief with a reproach: "Lord, if you had been here, my brother would not have died." Martha wanted only to have her brother alive again. Even though by bringing her brother back to life again Jesus gave Martha what she wanted, he could not wipe the sadness of death from her eyes completely, for raising Lazarus offered but a reprieve of the inevitable.

As we grow older, as friends and family precede us to the grave, the inevitability of death becomes more real. In quiet moments, thoughts of death that we keep at bay in the flurry of activity come crashing in upon us. Physician and poet William Carlos Williams, in his autobiographical short story "Danse Pseudomacabre," writes of such a moment. In the middle of the night, a phone call awakens a doctor. Sitting on the edge of his bed, looking at his wife fast asleep, he muses: "I have awakened with an overwhelming sense of death pressing my chest as if I had come reluctant from the grave to which a distorted homesickness continued to drag me, a sense of the end of everything. My wife lies asleep, curled against her pillow. Christ, Christ! How can I ever bear to be separated from this my boon companion, to be annihilated, to have her annihilated? How can a man live in the face of this daily uncertainty? How can a man not go mad with grief, with apprehension?" (88).

Our faith in the resurrection does not lessen the deep anxiety and sadness that attends upon thoughts of death but it does console us that death is not the final word on life; it does not annihilate us.

116 *Fifth Week of Lent*

Sunday

Cycle B: John 12: 20–33

Some Greeks approach Philip with the request, "Sir we want to see Jesus." Philip fetches Andrew, who introduces them to Jesus.

Some say that the most difficult instrument to play in a symphony orchestra is *second* violin. The apostle Andrew, who appears in today's gospel, played that part all of his life. New Testament lists of the apostles always refer to Andrew as "the brother of Peter" (Mt 10:2, Lk 6:14), as if his significance lies in his having a more distinguished brother. But Andrew had a distinguishing grace of his own. He introduced people to Jesus.[3]

Andrew appears three times in the New Testament, all in Saint John's gospel. He first appears when Jesus called him and John to be the first disciples. The early Church gave Andrew the title *Protokletos* (First-called). But no sooner had Andrew discovered Jesus, than he ran off and brought Peter, whereupon Jesus said, "You are Simon, son of John. You are to be called Cephas" (Jn 1: 42). As a reward for introducing Peter to Jesus, Andrew was "passed over" for a position of leadership. Few people could have borne such a situation with grace. Andrew did.

Next, Andrew appears in John 6, when Jesus multiplies the loaves and fishes. Andrew brought to Jesus the boy who had the two fish and some barley loaves. This seemingly insignificant event symbolizes an important belief. If we lay our gifts, talents, and possessions, however meager, at Jesus' feet, he can use them to perform miracles. Andrew understood this truth.

Finally, Andrew appears in the passage where some Greeks approach Philip with a request to have an audience with Jesus (Jn 12: 20–22). Philip was not sure what he should do. Jesus had just ridden triumphantly into Jerusalem, and the crowds were pressing around him. It was not a good time for a private interview. So Philip passed the request on to Andrew, who without any hesitation informed Jesus. Andrew's action indicates his belief in the universality of the gospel. It was not natural for a Jew to think of gentiles as being within the circumference of God's love. In fact, many rigid Jews considered gentiles accursed. But Andrew knew better, for he knew the heart of Jesus.

Sunday

Cycle C: John 8: 1–11

The Pharisees bring to Jesus a woman caught in the act of adultery to see if he will condemn her. Jesus simply says to them, "Let he who is without sin cast the first stone at her."

In John Cheever's short story "The Country Husband," Francis Weed is attending a cocktail party, when the maid serving the drinks arrests his attention. Francis had seen her before, when he was stationed in Trénon, France, at the end of World War II. She had been the subject of a public chastisement because she had lived with the German commandant during the Occupation.

> It was a cool morning in the fall. The sky was overcast and poured down onto the dirt crossroads a very discouraging light.... The prisoner arrived sitting on a three-legged stool in a farm cart. She stood by the cart while the mayor read the accusation and the sentence. Her head was bent ... [and] when the mayor was finished, she undid her hair ... and a little man with a gray mustache cut off her hair with shears and dropped it on the ground. Then, with a bowl of soapy

water and a straight razor, he shaved her skull clean. A woman approached and began to undo the fastenings of her clothes.... She [stood there] naked. The women jeered; the men were still ... the cold wind made her white skin rough and hardened the nipples of her breasts. The jeering ended gradually, put down by the recognition of their common humanity. (391)

When Jesus tells the scribes and Pharisees, "Let anyone among you who is without sin be the first to throw a stone at her," he invited them to recognize the common humanity that they shared with the woman. He didn't condemn the Pharisees and scribes any more than he condemned the woman. He simply bent down and gave them time to reflect upon their lives. We are told that they drifted away one by one, beginning with the oldest.

The judgment of the Pharisees and scribes was not *rash*, for the woman was guilty of adultery. Rather, it was *harsh*. But once they reflected upon their own sins and their desire for a merciful judgment from God, they could recognize their common, frail humanity in the shamed, guilt-ridden creature that stood before them. As their judgments softened, their clenched fists loosened and they released the stones they were holding.

Monday

John 8: 1–11

The Pharisees bring to Jesus a woman caught in the act of adultery. He does not condemn her but tells her to "Go your way, and from now on, do not sin again."

One danger our over-permissive society presents is to label the non-acceptance of any behavior as intolerant, judgmental, bigoted or close-minded. In *The Closing of the American Mind,* Allan Bloom questions this presupposition. *The* virtue that has dominated the American psyche for the past fifty years is what Bloom calls "openness." Openness assumes that truth is relative and that the relativity of truth is a moral postulate (25–43).

Fritz Perls expresses best the non-obligatory, unbinding moral stance of "openness" when he writes, "I'm not in this world to live up to your expectations and you're not in this world to live up to mine. You do your thing and I'll do mine. If by chance we meet then that's beautiful."

Allowing persons to "do their own thing" may not be judgmental, but it demonstrates neither compassion nor sound judgment. Such an attitude only results in children who never grow up, for they never had the need to develop self-discipline and self-control. Perls is right. We are not on this earth to live up to the expectations of others; nevertheless, adult relationships entail *legitimate* expectations and obligations.

Jesus treats the woman caught in adultery as an adult. He does not act either as a coercive or submissive parent; he neither accuses nor excuses, neither condemns her as a person nor condones her behavior.

We have no indication that Jesus forgave the woman her sin. To do so would have been presumptuous on his part, for he had no evidence that she was either remorseful or repentant. When Jesus said to her, "Go your way, and from now on, do not sin again," he was inviting her to examine her behavior and make a new beginning in her life. It was as if Jesus was saying to her, "Your life can be different if you want it to be. That's your choice."

Tuesday

John 8: 21–30

Only after Jesus is lifted up on the Cross will his adversaries realize that he was the Messiah.

"The suite was darkened. A nun with a holy face was nursing the man whose emaciated fingers stirred a rosary on the white sheet. He was still handsome and his voice summoned up a thick burr of individuality as he spoke to Dick. 'We get a lot of understanding at the end of life. Only now, Doctor Diver, do I realize what it was all about'" (249).

This passage, taken from the end of F. Scott Fitzgerald's last and most autobiographical novel, *Tender is the Night,* reflects the tragedy of Fitzgerald's life. Only toward the end of his life did Fitzgerald realize how much of it he had wasted. As he wrote four years before his untimely death in *The Crack-Up,* "I had been only a mediocre caretaker of most of the things left in my hands, even of my talent" (71)

"I am going away, and you will search for me, but you will die in your sin.... When you have lifted up the Son of Man, then you will realize that I am he." Jesus tells his adversaries that only *after* he is gone will they realize who he was. Missed opportunities, which have passed us by and will never come again, form the doleful note of regret that attends sin.

The Greek word for sin is *hamartia*, which literally means, "to miss the mark." Dying in one's sins means coming to the end of life and realizing that the meaning of life has been missed. And the sharpest pain of life's final regret is realizing that the purpose of our life was staring us in the face all along, but we were blind to it. When the Pharisees asked Jesus, "Who are you?" he responded, "What I have been telling you from the beginning."

All of us achieve a deeper understanding at the end of life. The stark contrast between *what is* and *what might have been*, the human being whom we have failed to become, stands in judgment upon our lives. From a human perspective, this is a moment of despair. What has been done cannot be undone. We cannot recall or relive a life of missed opportunities, arbitrary life choices, deadly compromise and concessions, trade-offs with the truth, and drifting with the current. But it can be a moment of salvation. Like the good thief, dying in his sins, we too can look upon the cross and beg for mercy and forgiveness.

Wednesday

John 8: 31–42

Jesus tells the Jewish authorities that being a true descendant of Abraham comes not from physical ancestry but from doing the will of God.

Justin Martyr wrote that some Jews who lived during the time of Jesus believed that because they were "descendants of Abraham according to the flesh [they would] certainly share in the eternal kingdom, even though they be faithless sinners and disobedient to God" (363). This may have

Fifth Week of Lent

been the reason, or one of the reasons why, when Jesus said that if they were slaves to sin then they had no "permanent place in the family," the people in today's gospel vehemently assert their descent from Abraham. It is worth noting that it was not his adversaries who lashed out at Jesus; rather, "those Jews who *believed in him*" did. Here we encounter a common dynamic of daily life, namely, how when we feel threatened our behavior toward others, even those who are close to us, can change in a moment.

Furthermore, today's gospel sets before us the vindictive venom that we can spew on others when we are either threatened or angry. When Jesus says to his audience that they are not Abraham's children, they fire back, "We are not illegitimate children!" This retort is retaliatory, for the original Greek contains the implication that "*we* are not illegitimate but *you are*."[4]

Because Mary had conceived out of wed-lock, Jesus was considered illegitimate. In Saint Mark's gospel, for example, the people of Jesus' hometown of Nazareth express their contempt of him by saying in derision, "Isn't this the carpenter, the son of Mary?" In the ancient world, a man was called by his mother's name only if he were illegitimate. One rumor said that a Roman soldier named Panthera was the father of Jesus.[5] The statement, "We are no illegitimate breed!" implies that the rumor of Jesus' illegitimacy was public knowledge and followed him wherever he went.

Like those in today's gospel, all of us are privy to the skeletons in other people's closets. We are keenly aware of the vulnerabilities of others and know where they are susceptible to shame and *how* to make them feel inferior. When threatened or angry, we can be tempted to attack where others are easily hurt. How often, in a moment of anger, have we dredged up a person's past and thrown it in his or her face? How often have we gone for the jugular because we felt defenseless? How often have we shamed someone to protect ourselves from being shamed?

Thursday

John 8: 51–59

Jesus' declaration, "Before Abraham came to be I AM," so enrages the Jewish authorities that they try to stone him.

"If I would say that I do not know him [God], I would be a liar like you." A liar not only tells an untruth but also hides the truth. Humanly speaking, it would have been to his advantage for Jesus to keep his unique relationship to God a secret. For Jesus' claim to divine sonship aroused the deep animosity in his opponents and eventually led to his death.

126   *Fifth Week of Lent*

We are tempted to conceal certain truths about ourselves for fear that we will be hated, judged rashly, or envied. For example, a highly educated person may be tempted to keep his accumulated knowledge well hidden, lest others think that he is making an ostentatious display of his learning. And while parading one's knowledge before others is an obvious form of pride, concealing it can be equally prideful. Take those, for example, who remain silent in every conversation because they want to project an aura of being more intelligent than they really are or to give the impression that they are "above" it all. We can use supercilious silence as a protective device. It can maintain an illusionary self-image of intellectual superiority or integrity while providing protection from being criticized or exposed as being ignorant or worse still — average.

We should determine what to lay bare and what to keep hidden about ourselves using criteria based on God's will. But to be ruled by this standard is exacting because of our strong fear that others will not think well of us. Also, the more we struggle to have humility rule both our speech and silence, the more we become conscious that some form of pride lurks in both.

One of the most difficult paradoxes to manage in the spiritual life is to grow in self-knowledge while forgetting oneself. We need to grow constantly in insight, for blindness keeps us trapped in endless cycles of self-destructive behavior. Yet always looking at ourselves and dissecting our motives poses the danger that our minds can revolve around our selves endlessly like a ponderous millstone. We need to take ourselves seriously in a lighthearted way.

Friday

John 10: 31–42

The Jewish authorities try to arrest Jesus for blasphemy because he made himself equal to God.

At best, this is a difficult gospel passage to understand. As a believing Christian, I struggle with it. On one hand, I believe Jesus' assertion that the unbelief of many of his opponents was willful and culpable. Yet, had I lived in Palestine during the time of Jesus, I may not have thought that Jesus had blasphemed, but I certainly would have questioned his sanity. Who but a madman would make himself out to be God? There are many such claimants on psychiatric wards.

Today's gospel underlines the mystery of the gift of faith. Some of the Jews wanted to stone Jesus, but others came to believe in him. Faith is a pure gift from God. Therefore, we cannot judge a person's lack of faith. Some are agnostic or atheistic through no fault of their own. Conversely, while there can be more faith in honest doubt than in half the creeds, as Tennyson puts it, we should not presume that all doubt and lack of faith are come by honestly. Faith can be lost or never accepted through our own fault. C. S. Lewis wrote:

> The man who is deliberately trying not to know whether Christianity is true or false, because he foresees endless trouble if it should turn out to be true ... is like the man who deliberately "forgets" to look at the notice board because, if he did, he might find his name down for some unpleasant duty. He is like the man who won't look at his bank account because he's afraid of what he might find there. He is like the man who won't go to the doctor when he first feels a mysterious pain, because he is afraid of what the doctor may tell him. The man who remains an unbeliever for such reasons is not in a state of honest error.... [This is evading God]. It is look[ing] the other way, pretend[ing] you haven't noticed, it is leaving the receiver off the telephone because it might be He who was ringing up, it is leaving unopened certain letters in a strange handwriting because they might be from Him. ("Man or Rabbit?" 111)

Some people do lose their faith as the result of honest inquiry and others because of scandal in the Church. But I am more inclined to believe that most people lose their faith through neglect. Faith often dies a quiet, unattended, unnoticed death because it hasn't been fed. Unpraying, un-resisting, without moral resolve, we can easily drift away from what we once so ardently believed. Often, it happens imperceptibly. How culpable a person is for such a loss — only God knows.

Saturday

John 11: 45–57

Caiphas proposes to the Sanhedrin that it is better for one man to die than that the whole nation perish.

The connotation of the Greek phrase translated "What are we to do?" suggests helplessness. The Greek might better be rendered, "What *can* we do?" It is as if the members of the Sanhedrin are saying, "What if the people get caught up in this new movement and it spins out of control? Rome would come in and crush our nation. We have to do something about Jesus, but what *can* we do? His popularity is growing and growing. And now with him raising a man from the dead...." The Sanhedrin has a national security crisis on its hands, and they don't know what to do about it. Within this context the Sanhedrin accepts Caiphas's extreme proposal to have Jesus killed. The members of the Sanhedrin were all too willing to hand over their dilemma to Caiphas. Likewise, when we are threatened and feel powerless to protect ourselves, we will go along with courses of action that in normal circumstances we would reject outright.

We have a deep ambivalence regarding freedom. We want to be free to make our own choices, but we also want to be relieved of the burden of responsibility. We are like adolescents who one day says to a parent, "Don't tell me what to do, I'm old enough to make my own decisions," but the next day, anxiously seeks advice regarding what to do.

Dostoevsky wrote, "Man has no more pressing, agonizing need than the need to find someone to whom he can hand over as quickly as possible the gift of freedom" (306). This temptation strengthens when we are frightened and feel helpless to extricate ourselves from our fear; when we are afraid, all we want is to feel safe. At such moments, it takes great courage not to take the easy way out or to accept an expedient solution.

Shortly after Khrushchev rose to power, he was giving a speech denouncing the cruelty Stalin inflicted upon the Russian people. From the back of the hall, someone shouted, "Where were you when Stalin was killing all those innocent people?" Khrushchev demanded that the man reveal himself. Silence fell upon the crowd. Khrushchev said, "Where was I when Stalin killed all those people? The same place that you are now — hiding behind silence."

All of us have been tempted to abdicate responsibility under the cloak of silence. But sometimes God calls us to be the one dissenting voice in a crowd.

Holy Week

Palm Sunday

Cycle A: Matthew 26: 14 –27, 66

Today's gospel is the Passion according to Saint Matthew.

The souls in the Vestibule of Dante's *Inferno* are rejected by both heaven and hell, loathsome to both God and God's enemies. These souls cannot die because they never lived. Commonly, they have been referred to as "the opportunists," or "the neutrals" because they never took a stand in life. Their motto is, "Safety first and safety last." They never took a position on any issue or allied themselves with any group lest one day they find themselves on the losing side. Dante describes one of these souls as "the coward who made the great refusal" (III.60). While Dante scholars have never reached consensus about the identity of this soul the most likely candidate is Pontius Pilate.[6]

Pilate's great refusal was his decision to abdicate his authority and allow an innocent man to be executed. His sin was moral cowardice. Because it was politically expedient, he washed his hands of an awkward situation. He passed the buck to the crowd.

Pilate gambled with a man's life and lost. We are told Pilate realized that the Jewish leaders had handed Jesus over to him out of jealousy. He was banking that the crowd did not share the leaders' animosity, for a few days earlier he had seen the crowd's enthusiasm when Jesus had made his entry into Jerusalem.

Pilate concocted a clever plot. By allowing the crowd to make the decision whether to release Jesus, he didn't have to violate his own conscience by condemning a man he knew to be innocent, and at the same time he could throw up his hands and say to the leaders, "Well, your own people have spoken; it's their decision."

When Pilate's scheme backfired, he washed his hands and declared himself innocent. But in truth, he washed his hands in blood. Pilate knew what he had done. And even worse, he realized that he had the power to prevent it. Pilate's refusal to make a choice *was* his choice. His cautious cowardice proved deadly, not only for Jesus but also for himself. How can someone live with himself knowing that he had caused the death of an innocent man?

We know little about Pilate once he walked off the pages of the gospels. Historians paint him as a well-meaning but ineffectual leader. Unable to suppress a revolt in Palestine, Pilate was called back to Rome. Relieved of his commission, he was exiled to Gaul, where he committed suicide.

In James R. Mills' novel, *The Memoirs of Pontius Pilate,* we find Pilate in exile, haunted by all the men whom he had ordered to be executed, espe-

136

cially Jesus. I would like to believe that before he took own his life, Pilate's troubled soul found peace in the words that Jesus spoke upon the Cross: "Father, forgive them for they know not what they do."

Sunday

Cycle B: Mark 11: 1–10

Saint Mark's rendition of the triumphant procession into Jerusalem emphasizes Jesus as a humble messiah.

The ashes placed upon our foreheads on Ash Wednesday do not have a single meaning. They can symbolize our mortality ("Remember that you are dust and to dust you shall return") or our need for conversion ("Repent, and believe in the gospel"). The ashes may also represent illusionary dreams that have come to nothing, for they are derived from the palms that we carry in procession on Palm Sunday.

On the first Palm Sunday, the people lined the streets to cheer as they welcomed Jesus into Jerusalem as a conquering hero, their messiah, who they believed would free them from the tyranny of Rome. They were blind to the meaning of the prophetic sign of a king astride a beast of burden, a symbol of a humble, peaceful, monarch. In T.S. Eliot's words, "We had the experience but missed the meaning" ("The Dry Salvages," 39).

We too misconstrue the events of our lives because we interpret them through the lenses of our needs and desires. Like the people in today's gospel, we can project our need for deliverance upon others. For example, the desire to possess the perfect mate who will eradicate all loneliness can transform a person in one's imagination into a god or goddess. But all our gods and goddesses are mere mortals. And when they disappoint us, we cast them down from their thrones. Our cheers of "hosanna" quickly become jeers of "Crucify him. Crucify him."

So many relationships collapse and fall asunder because they are built on sand. Aristotle believed that true friendship is rare, that is, a relationship based upon desiring the Good for the other. Unfortunately, he wrote, the majority of what people call "friendship" is not friendship at all, but a relationship of convenience or self-seeking in which a person is pursuing his own advantage. "That is why they fall in and out of friendship quickly, changing their attitude often within the same day" (263).

How many times have we believed people to be our "friends" only to discover that we were being used? How often have we used people in the same way?

Sunday

Cycle C: Luke 22: 14 – 23, 56

Today's gospel is the Passion according to Saint Luke.

One of the priests executed during the Mexican Revolution was Miguel Pro. A famous photograph of his execution shows him with his arms outstretched in the form of a cross. The government took the photograph, mass produced it, and distributed it among the people as a means of both mocking the Church and showing the people who was in charge. But within a year, the government banned the photo because it had become an icon of adoration among the Mexican people.

Where does real power reside? Pilate's statement, "Do you not know that *I have the power* to release you, and the power to crucify you" is an illusion, for Jesus laid down his life of his own free will. At times, power seems to lie in the hands of the rulers of this world, but in due time, the truth emerges that it lies in the hands of God.

One of the truths embedded in the Passion of Jesus is that the reality of any given situation comes to light in God's time. What looked like defeat on Good Friday was disclosed as the triumph of God's love on Easter Sunday. The import of this truth for our lives is that no act of love is ever wasted. Every time we do the will of God, in spite of all appearances, we contribute to the redemption of the world. We may never see the positive impact of our good deeds; nevertheless, if they are acts of Love they are guaranteed by God.

"Love," writes Evelyn Underhill, "after all, makes the whole difference between an execution and a martyrdom" (55). If the Crucifixion had not been an act of Divine Love, it would have been no more than a routine execution in a remote corner of the Roman Empire.

The same is true with us. Because we are members of the Body of Christ, whenever we unite our actions with Christ upon the Cross, they are redemptive. Love transforms the banal actions of daily life into divine deeds that plant the seeds of God's transforming love in our world.

Monday

Mary, the sister of Lazarus, anoints the feet of Jesus but Judas protests that the oil could have been sold and the proceeds given to the poor.

Picture yourself on a beautiful summer evening, sitting around in lawn chairs in your back yard, talking with friends. As dusk descends you do not notice the fading light because your eyes adjust automatically to the gradual waning of the day. This illustrates how we can change gradually without noticing it.

It seems almost inconceivable that Judas, an intimate of Jesus, could betray him for a pittance. But we are told that "[Judas] was a thief; he kept the common purse and used to steal what was put into it." In short, stealing had become a habit with him. As the habit of stealing gradually grew, Judas' conscience deadened as he rationalized why what he was doing "wasn't so bad."

In *Paradise Lost,* Satan slips into paradise during the evening twilight. "Twilight ... the short arbiter twixt day and night" (IX, 50). Symbolically, Milton is representing the deadly process of arbitration that we enter into when we allow our conscience to make concessions. As the darkness of evil gradually and imperceptibly settles over our lives, we do not notice what is happening until it is too late.

Allegedly, when Leonardo da Vinci painted *The Last Supper* he searched for models whose faces depicted his conceptions of each disciple. One Sunday, when da Vinci was attending Mass in the Milan Cathedral, he spied a young man in the choir whose countenance captured da Vinci's ideal image of Christ. The young man's face embodied innocence, compassion, love, and tenderness.

Many years later, da Vinci had only one more disciple to paint — Judas. To find a man whose face would reflect deceit, avarice, a life of sin and despair, da Vinci scoured the prisons of Milan. There he found his subject, a man whose hardened features reflected a life of crime.

As the man was sitting in da Vinci's studio to be painted, he began to cry. When the master asked him what was the matter, the poor wretch said, "Maestro, don't you recognize me? I sat for you many years ago. I was the young man you painted to represent Jesus."

It is frightening that often we do not recognize the most drastic change in character that takes place within us until *after* it has been accomplished. Judas did not realize that whatever he stole from the common purse, he stole from himself. He robbed himself of his own humanity. The same is true with us. There is no such thing as "petty" theft, for no loss of soul is inconsequential.

Tuesday

John 13: 21–33,36–38

At the Last Supper, Jesus predicts that he
will be betrayed by one of his disciples.

At the Last Supper, Jesus knew who was about
to betray him, so he dipped a morsel of bread in a
dish and handed it to Judas, a gesture reserved for
honored guests. In different ways, all of us have experienced this gesture from Jesus. Call to mind a
time in your life that you were on the brink of be-
traying God but at the last moment decided
against it. Now, try to recall what made you
change your mind. Perhaps someone made a remark that made you realize the serious consequences that would follow in the wake of your
choice. Or perhaps a passage of scripture, a line of
poetry, or a memory from childhood that came
unbidden to your mind provided the means of
your salvation.

We find an example of one such morsel of di-
vine grace given at a critical crossroads of life in
Michael Goldberg's book *Namesake*. Goldberg's
lifelong obsession was to track down and murder
Klaus Barbie, the man personally responsible for
the execution of Goldberg's father during World
War II. After years of pursuing the infamous
Nazi war criminal, Goldberg finally cornered

him. And as Goldberg was about to kill Barbie, an old Jewish proverb began to repeat itself in his mind. "Every murder is a suicide." Goldberg let Barbie go. Upon reflection, Goldberg realized that his decision not to kill Barbie had been his salvation. It freed him from his lifelong obsession to kill a Nazi. He accomplished this goal, but not in the manner he had intended. He killed the Nazi that lived within his own heart.

All of us have stood at the precipice of a self-destructive choice. At such moments, God offers us morsels of divine grace, warning us not to take that fatal next step. Even if we ignore God's invitation of grace, God still offers us salvation in the form of forgiveness.

Judas rejected Jesus' invitation and eventually hanged himself. But we do not know his final fate, for the offer of God's forgiveness was as present to Judas at the moment of his death as it was when Jesus handed him the morsel of bread at the Last Supper.

Wednesday

Matthew 26: 14–25

Judas asks the Jewish authorities, "What are you willing to give me if I hand Jesus over to you?" Jesus predicts his betrayal at the Last Supper.

In Frank Stockton's fable "The Lady, or the Tiger?" we see how savage possessive love and jealousy can be. The story is set in ancient times, in a country where a semi-barbaric king has devised an ingenious method for determining a man's guilt or innocence. The king built an enormous amphitheater with a door on one side of the arena and two doors on the opposite. The accused would enter through the single door, walk to the other side, and stand before one of the other two doors. Behind one was a hungry tiger; behind the other a beautiful young maiden. The accused had to open one of the doors. If he chose the door that concealed the tiger, the beast would devour him instantly. If he opened the other, he received the beautiful maiden as his bride.

It so happened that the daughter of the king had fallen in love with one of her courtiers, and he had fallen in love with the princess. They professed their love to one another, but it proved ill fated, for the affair became known to the king.

Since it was a crime for a commoner to fall in love with the princess, the man was condemned to the arena.

But the princess was clever. She found out by trickery which door concealed the lady and which concealed the tiger. And her lover knew that she would obtain this information. So when he entered the arena, he glanced over to catch some sign as to which door he should open. The princess did give a sign. She raised her right hand slowly and with a slight movement that only her lover could see, she motioned to the right. The youth smiled in relief and opened the door on the right.

Did the princess send her lover to certain death or to marital bliss? We might presume the latter, but should not judge too hastily. When the princess found out which door concealed the lady, she also discovered *who* the lady was — a damsel of the court, a maiden of peerless beauty, whom the princess had often seen throwing glances of admiration upon her lover. Also, the princess perceived or thought she had perceived that these glances were returned. She had often seen them talking together, which filled her with jealous rage. She hated the woman behind the door and could not bear the thought of this creature she loathed being wed to the man the princess loved. But could the princess send her lover to certain death? Now, what greeted the man when he opened the door on the right — the lady, or the tiger? Stockton ends the story with this question.

Jealousy is fierce and barbaric. It will destroy what it loves rather than surrender it to a hated foe. The factors of jealousy and hatred can help us to understand the betrayal of Judas. William Barclay writes, "Judas was the only non-Galilean in the apostolic band, the man who was different. Perhaps from the beginning he had the feeling that he was the odd man out. There may have been in him a certain frustrated ambition.... He clearly held a very important position [among the apostles]. He was the treasurer of the company....There can be no doubt that Judas held a high place among the twelve — and yet he was not one of the intimate three — Peter, James, and John.... It is not difficult to see him, even if he had a very high place among the twelve, slowly and unreasonably growing jealous and embittered because others had a still higher place. And it is not difficult to see that bitterness coming to obsess him, until in the end his love turned to hate and he betrayed Jesus" (76–77).

Jealousy can be frightening in its intensity, and triangular relationships can be the most corrosive and destructive forces in our lives. The deadly venom of jealousy can destroy those around us and eat us up inside. Shakespeare was right. The green-eyed monster "mock[s] the meat it feeds on" (*Othello* 3.3.166–67). It devoured Judas and can do the same to us.

Holy Thursday

John 13: 1–15

On the night before he died, Jesus washed the feet of his disciples and said to them, "I have set you an example, that you also should do as I have done to you."

The institution of the Eucharist is a central aspect of the celebration of Holy Thursday, but it is not the only one. The Church's selection of the gospel reading makes this evident. It does not even mention the Eucharist. Rather, it focuses on the last will and testimony of a man about to die.

Jesus wanted to say many things at the Last Supper, but had so little time to say them. He had taught his disciples many truths. Now, as he was about to depart from this earth, he had to select carefully what he wanted them to remember the most. Jesus accomplished this task in a single action — washing the feet of his disciples.

John Chrysostom writes that by washing their feet Jesus taught his disciples a two-fold truth. First, they were "not to exalt themselves one above the other, and say as they had before, 'Who is the greatest'" ("Homilies on the Gospel of John and Hebrews" 260). Leaders of the Church must demonstrate humility because few things have done more damage to the credibility

Holy Week

of the gospel than the haughty arrogance and luxurious lifestyles of the clergy. Augustine, in extremely strong language, describes the effect that shepherds can have on their sheep. By the wicked lives and bad example of shepherds the sheep are *killed.* They kill their sheep's souls, for when they see how their shepherd behaves they say in their heart, "If my pastor lives like that, why should not I live like him?" ("From a Sermon on Pastors" 271).

The way that we live influences people. In this regard, all of us are shepherds of souls. Our influence can be negative like the bad shepherds Augustine describes, or positive. In this regard, Saint Teresa writes, "When virtue is placed before our eyes, the one who desires it grows fond of it and seeks to gain it" ("The Way of Perfection" 62). There is no such thing as a solitary sin; virtue and vice are not private affairs, for directly or indirectly our actions affect people. John Chrysostom describes a second truth that Jesus wanted to communicate to his disciples by washing their feet — humble deeds of love proclaim more than words ("Homilies on the Gospel of John and Hebrews" 260). Daily life confirms this truth; what people do affects us more than what they say. In washing his disciples' feet, Jesus sets before us the essence of his teaching in all its divine simplicity — love one another.

Good Friday

John 18: 1–19, 42

The Passion of Our Lord Jesus Christ according to Saint John.

In Ernest Hemingway's short story "Today is Friday," three Roman soldiers are unwinding in a Jerusalem bar on a Friday night. It had been a long, hard week. It was Passover, which meant that they had worked double shifts because of the crowds. And to make things worse, a would-be Messiah named Jesus had ridden into Jerusalem the previous Sunday and almost caused a riot. But everything had taken care of itself. Passover was coming to an end, and when Jesus was crucified his disciples dispersed.

While downing their drinks, two soldiers are talking about their day's work.

> *1ˢᵗ Soldier*: Ain't I seen 'em? I seen plenty of them [crucified]. I tell you [Jesus] was pretty good in there today.

> *2ⁿᵈ Soldier*: You're a regular Christer, big boy.

> *1ˢᵗ Soldier:* Sure, go on and kid him. But listen wile I tell you something. He was pretty good in there today. (210)

A third soldier remains quiet. He is sick. He had seen just as many crucifixions as the other two, but somehow this one had been different. He cannot put into words how it was different or what he had seen but it had made him sick. The story ends with the soldiers going back to the barracks and one of them saying to his sick comrade, "You been out here too long. That's all."

Hemingway's story reveals one of the ways in which God's grace breaks into our lives. When we have a new reaction to a routine experience, when we see the old and the ordinary in a new light, we experience revelation. Like the soldier in the story, we may not be able to put into words what is happening to us, but revelation happens not in the explanation so much as in our awareness. How often do we become sick because the tenderness of God's love exposes the callousness of our lives? At such moments, we can be tempted to say to ourselves something like the soldier said to his comrade. "I've been working too hard." Or "I'm taking myself too seriously." We can readily dismiss feelings of uneasiness or guilt over a long-standing behavior as nothing but merely a passing mood, when in fact, however, such feelings may contain a divine invitation.

Holy Saturday

When Dante and Virgil reach the deepest pit of hell, located at the center of the earth, they begin to climb upwards because gravity has been reversed. This image symbolizes many truths. One is that when a great reversal takes place in our lives, we are not immediately aware of it. Dante and Virgil are still groping in the darkness, but they have reversed their course and are heading toward the light.

Holy Saturday represents those times when a great change has taken place in our lives but we are not yet aware of it. For example, after a deflating blow, often it takes our egos days, months and even years to begin to experience the deep peace of humility that the shattering event has caused. At first we feel only the death throes of what we have called our life — numbness, anger, anxiety, depression. But once the waves have subsided, there emerges the indescribable serenity of the Real Self.

Holy Saturday is like a seed that has broken open in the ground but has not yet broken through to the surface. The growth that lies in darkness has not yet reached the light of consciousness. And when it finally breaks through to the surface, the effect is often so gentle that we don't even recognize its presence. This is true regarding various transformations in our lives. C. S. Lewis, for example, compares his experience of coming to believe in Jesus Christ as "when a man, after long sleep, still lying motionless in bed, becomes aware that he is now awake" (*Surprised by Joy* 237). Lewis had spent many years reading, thinking, inwardly wrestling with and outwardly debating the existence of God and the claims of Christianity, but when the gift of faith finally arrived, he was not engaged in thinking about God nor did he feel deep emotion. Suddenly, he was conscious that faith *had* been given to him. The moment of transformation comes not with a thunderclap but as a gentle rain falling upon our parched, wearied, and wounded souls — unannounced. Carl Jung once said that when healing arrives, only one word can express its epiphany — miraculous. One moment, something struggled with for years is torturing a person, and the next moment it is gone. Psychiatrist Theodore I. Rubin relates how a great personal failure threw him into a pit of depression and self-hate. He could not turn off the self-hating machinery of his mind and spent sleepless hours of self-torturing ruminations. He sought professional help and struggled with his demons to no avail, until one night before going to sleep he decided with his heart, "Leave it all be.... That night I slept peacefully. In the morning my depression was gone" (4–5). We experience such miraculous healings in many other ways. For example, one day we discover that certain people or situations that had imprisoned us for years no longer provoke us to fear or rage. Or we respond with joyous alacrity to requests that we had previously done so grudgingly. At such times, we don't know how the change has taken place or even when it came about. All we know is that the whole inner atmosphere of our soul has been changed. As Saint Teresa once said, often we receive the fruits of our labors all at once.

Holy Saturday, writes Karl Rahner, "is a symbol of everyday life" (24). It expresses the growth that accrues hidden in the darkness of our souls and resurrects in God's time.

Easter Vigil

Mark 16: 1–8

Women come to the tomb of Jesus to anoint his body, but he is not there. Instead, an angel tells them, "Do not be alarmed ... he is not here, he has been raised." But they flee in fear and bewilderment.

In Leonid Andreyev's short story "Lazarus," many people came to see the man who had been raised from the dead. After they have seen Lazarus, however, they wished that they had not. When they peered into his eyes, they peered into the cold, blackness of the grave. They saw nothing except hideous death grinning back at them mockingly. Raising Lazarus from the dead was not a resurrection to new life but the resuscitation of a corpse. Andreyev's story answers the question posed to us in the *Exultet* at the Easter Vigil. "What good would life have been to us, had Christ not come as our Redeemer?" Nothing! If the darkness of death is the last and irrevocable word on life, then does life have any ultimate meaning? If this earth is a dead-end street, then life is a journey going nowhere.

A few months before he died, C. S. Lewis wrote the following in a letter to a friend: "Think of yourself as a seed patiently wintering in the earth; waiting to come up a flower in the Gardener's good time, up into the *real* world, the real waking. I suppose that our whole present life, looked back on from there, will seem only a drowsy half-waking. We are here in the land of dreams. But cockcrow is coming. It is nearer now than when I began this letter" (*An Anthology of C. S. Lewis: A Mind Awake* 187).

Saint Mark's gospel ends with the story of the empty tomb (16:1– 8).[7] In this passage, the women encounter not the resurrected Christ but the empty shell of death that points beyond this world, an empty tomb that cannot hold captive the Author of Life. At the Easter Virgil, we stand in darkness, like the women who stood before the empty tomb. All we know at this point is that, "He is not here," and must await the proclamation, "He is risen!"

Notes

1. I cannot take credit for this illustration. I heard it many years ago on an audiotape given by a person whose name I am unable to recall.

2. For insightful psychological analysis of the relationships between the quests for power, prestige and possessions as means of reassurance against helplessness, humiliation and destitution, respectively see chapter ten of Karen Horney's *The Neurotic Personality of Our Times* (New York: Norton Press, 1937), 138–159.

3. I owe these ideas about Andrew to William Barclay. See his book, *The Master's Men* (Nashville: Abingdon Press, 1959), 40–46.

4. For a good treatment of the rumors concerning Jesus' illegitimacy that circulated during his lifetime, see Raymond Brown's commentary on Saint John's Gospel in the Anchor Bible series (Vol. 1, 357).

5. In his polemical work *Contra Celsum,* the third century theologian Origen refutes this allegation.

6. The other most likely candidate to have "made the great denial" is Pope Celestine V who resigned the papacy in 1294, allowing Dante's enemy Boniface VIII to ascend the papal throne.

7. More than a century after Mark's gospel was written, a second ending was added (16: 9–20).

Works Cited

Abbé de Tourville, *Letters of Direction*. Wilton, CT: Morehouse Barlow, 1939.

Aristotle. The *Nicomachean Ethics*. Translated by. J. A. K. Thomson. New York: Penguin, 1976.

Augustine. "From a Sermon on Pastors." In *The Liturgy of the Hours, Vol. 4.*, 271. New York: Catholic Book Publishing, 1975.

_____. "The Lord's Sermon on the Mount." In *Ancient Christian Writers*, translated by John J. Jepson, S.S., 92. Westminster, MD: Newman Press, 1948.

Barclay, William. *The Master's Men*. Nashville, TN: Abingdon Press, 1959.

Blake, William. "A Poison Tree." In *The Complete Poems*, 129-30. New York: Penguin, 1988.

Bloom, Allan. *The Closing of the American Mind*. New York: Touchstone, 1987.

Bolt, Robert. *A Man for All Seasons*. New York: Vintage, 1962.

Cheever, John. "The Country Husband." In *The Stories of John Cheever*, 391. New York: Ballantine, 1978.

Clément, Olivier. *The Roots of Christian Mysticism*. Translated by Theodore Berkeley, O.C.S.O. Hyde Park, NY: New City Press, 1995.

Climacus, John. *The Ladder of Divine Ascent*. Translated by Colum Luibheid and Norman Russell. New York: Paulist Press, 1982.

Coles, Robert. *The Call of Stories: Teaching and the Moral Imagination*. Boston: Houghton Mifflin, 1989.

_____. *Dorothy Day: A Radical Devotion*. Reading, MA: Addison-Wesley, 1987.

Dickens, Charles. *A Christmas Carol*. New York: Dove, 1991.

_____. *Great Expectation*. New York: Penguin, 1996

_____. *A Tale of Two Cities*. New York: Penguin, 2000.

Dorotheos of Gaza. *Discourses and Sayings*. Translated by Eric P. Wheeler. Kalamazoo, MI: Cistercian Publications, 1977.

Dostoevsky, Fyodor. *The Brothers Karamazov*. Translated by Andrew R. MacAndrew. New York: Bantam, 1970.

Eliot, T. S. "The Dry Salvages." In *Four Quartets*, 39. New York: Harcourt, Brace, Jovanovich, 1971.

_____. "Little Gidding." In *Four Quartets*, 54. New York: Harcourt, Brace, Jovanovich, 1971.

_____. *Murder in the Cathedral*. New York: Harcourt, Brace, Jovanovich, 1963.

_____. "The Waste Land." In *Selected Poems*, 51. New York: Harcourt, Brace, Jovanovich, 1964.

Fitzgerald, F. Scott. *The Crack-Up*. Edited by Edmund Wilson. New York: New Directions, 1993.

_____. *Tender is the Night*. New York: Simon and Schuster, 1962.

Francis de Sales. *Introduction to the Devout Life*. Translated by Michael Day, Cong. Orat. Wheathampstead, Herts.: Anthony Clarke, 1990.

Frankl, Viktor. *The Doctor and The Soul*. Translated by Richard and Clara Winston. New York: Alfred A. Knopf, 1965.

_____ . *Man's Search for Meaning.* Translated by Ilse Lasch. New York: Pocket Books, 1963.

Gregory the Great. *Pastoral Care.* Westminster, MD: Newman Press, 1950.

Herbert, George. "The Pulley." In *George Herbert: The Country Parson, The Temple*, edited by John N. Wall, Jr., 284. New York: Paulist Press, 1981.

Hemingway, Ernest. "Today is Friday." In *Men without Women,* 210. New York: Charles Scribner's Sons, 1955.

Jerome. "The Letters of St. Jerome Vol. 1." In *Ancient Christian Writers,* translated by Charles Christopher Mierow, 160-61. Westminster, MD: Newman Press, 1963.

John of the Cross. "The Ascent of Mount Carmel." In *The Collected Works of St. John of the Cross,* translated by Otilio Rodriguez, O.C.D. and Kieran Kavanaugh, O.C.D., 132. Washington, D.C.: ICS Publications, 1991.

John Chrysostom. "Homilies on the Gospel of John and Hebrews." In *The Nicene and Post-Nicene Fathers of The Christian Church, Vol. XIV,* edited by Philip Schaff, 260. Grand Rapids, MI: Wm. B. Eerdmans, 1956.

_____ . "Homilies on the Gospel of Saint Matthew." In *The Nicene and Post-Nicene Fathers of The Christian Church, Vol. 10,* edited by Philip Schaff, 132. Grand Rapids, MI: Wm. B. Eerdmans, 1956.

Julian of Norwich. *Showings.* Translated by Edmund Colledge, O.S.A. and James Walsh, S.J. New York: Paulist Press, 1978).

Justin Martyr. "Dialogue with Trypho." In *Writings of Saint Justin Martyr,* translated by Thomas B. Falls, 363. New York: Christian Heritage, 1948.

Levinson, Daniel. *The Seasons of a Man's Life.* New York: Ballantine, 1978.

Lewis, C.S. *An Anthology of C. S. Lewis: A Mind Awake.* Edited by Clyde S. Kirby. New York: Harcourt Brace Jovanovich, 1968.

_____ . *A Grief Observed.* New York: Bantam, 1961.

_____ . " Man or Rabbit?" In *God in the Dock: Essays on Theology and Ethics*, edited by. Walter Hooper, 111. Grand Rapids, MI: William B. Eerdmans, 1970.

_____ . *Reflections on the Psalms.* New York: Harcourt, Brace, Jovanovich, 1958.

_____ . *The Screwtape Letters.* New York: Macmillan, 1961.

_____ . *Surprised by Joy: The Shape of My Early Life.* New York: Harcourt, Brace, and World, 1955.

Luke, Helen. "Frodo's Mithril Coat in *The Lord of the Rings*." In *The Inner Story*: *Myth and Symbol in the Bible and Literature*, 75-6. New York: Crossroads, 1982

Maugham, Somerset. *Of Human Bondage.* Garden City, NJ: Sun Dial Press,1936.

Merton, Thomas. *The Wisdom of the Desert.* New York: New Directions, 1960.

Missildine, W. Hugh. *The Inner Child of the Past.* New York: Pocket Books, 1963.

Muggeridge, Malcolm. *Jesus Rediscovered.* Garden City, NJ: Doubleday, 1969.

Newman, John Henry. "The Ventures of Faith." In *Parochial and Plain Sermons,* Vol. 4, 299. New York: Scribner, Welford, 1868.

O'Connor, Flannery. *Letters of Flannery O'Connor: The Habit of Being.* Edited by Sally Fitzgerald. New York: Farrar, Straus, Giroux, 1979.

Powers, Jessica. "Abraham." In *The Selected Poetry of Jessica Powers*. Edited by Regina Siefgried and Robert Morneau, 66. Washington, D.C. ICS Publications, 2000.

Rahner, Karl. "Passion of the Son of Man: Words for Holy Week." In *Grace in Freedom*, 124. New York: Herder and Herder, 1969.

Rubin, Theodore I. *Compassion and Self-Hate: An Alternative to Despair*. New York: David McKay Company, 1975.

　　The Sayings of the Desert Fathers. Translated by Benedicta Ward, SLG. London: A. R. Mowbray, 1975.

Shaffer, Peter. *Amadeus*. New York: New American Library, 1981.

Sheed, Wilfred. *In Love with Daylight: A Memoir of Recovery*. Pleasantville, N.Y.: Akadine Press, 1995.

Teresa of Avila. "The Book of Her Foundations." In *The Collected Works of St. Teresa of Avila*, vol. 3, translated by Otilio Rodriguez, O.C.D. and Kieran Kavanaugh, O.C.D., 140. Washington, D.C.: ICS Publications, 1980.

　　. "The Interior Castle." In *The Collected Works of St. Teresa of Avila*, vol.2, translated by Otilio Rodriguez, O.C.D. and Kieran Kavanaugh, O.C.D., 444. Washington, D.C.: ICS Publications, 1980.

　　. "Meditations on the Song of Songs." In *The Collected Works of St. Teresa of Avila*, vol.2, translated by Otilio Rodriguez, O.C.D. and Kieran Kavanaugh, O.C.D., 256. Washington, D.C.: ICS Publications, 1980.

　　. "The Way of Perfection." In *The Collected Works of St. Teresa of Avila*, vol.2, translated by Otilio Rodriguez, O.C.D. and Kieran Kavanaugh, O.C.D., 97. Washington, D.C.: ICS Publications, 1980.

Thérèse of Lisieux. *St. Thérèse of Lisieux: By Those Who Knew Her*. Edited and translated by Christopher O'Mahony. Dublin: Veritas, 1982

　　. *Story of a Soul*. Translated by John Clarke, O.C.D. Washington, D.C.: ICS Publications, 1999.

Thoreau, Henry David. "Walden." In *Walden and Other Writings*, 86. New York: The Modern Library, 1965.

Tolkien, J.R.R. *The Letters of J.R.R. Tolkien*. Edited by Humphrey Carpenter. Boston: Houghton Mifflin, 1981.

Underhill, Evelyn. *The School of Charity*. Harrisburg, PA: Morehouse Publishing: 1991.

Wilder, Thornton. "The Angel that Troubled the Waters." In *The Angel that Troubled the Waters and Other Plays,* 146-48. New York: Coward- McCann, 1928

Williams, William Carlos. "Danse Pseudomacabre" In *The Doctor Stories*, 88. New York: New Direction, 1962.

160